THE BEAST

A CHILLING TRUE STORY OF A PSYCHOPATHIC CHILD KILLER

RYAN GREEN

For Helen, Harvey, Frankie and Dougie

Disclaimer

This book is about real people committing real crimes. The story has been constructed by facts but some of the scenes, dialogue and characters have been fictionalised.

Polite Note to the Reader

This book is written in British English except where fidelity to other languages or accents are appropriate. Some words and phrases may differ from US English.

YOUR FREE BOOK IS WAITING

CONTENTS

Summer Shining Like Gold

There was just something about Clifford. He seemed to walk to a different beat as he strolled down the street. Like everyone else was trailing along the ground and he was floating, with a band playing his theme song in the background. When people got close to him, stepping inside that cloud of expensive cigar smoke that followed him everywhere he went, there was a moment when they could almost hear it. The distant hint of music on the wind.

Some people called it charisma, and they loved him for it, but even the people who didn't love him found themselves caught up in it. Like this was all his story and they were just bit-part characters.

Working inwards from the thick blue smoke, there were more colours to see, bright custom suits and silk shirts, things that would have looked garish or comical on anyone else but seemed like the perfect fit for Clifford. Every line tailored to his body, every colour offsetting the natural ruddiness of his skin. If somebody took the time to stare for long enough, the body beneath the suit could be made out, the camouflage penetrated and the thick-necked potato-shaped physique underneath all that expensive tailoring made visible. The truth beneath the lie of humanity, some great lumbering ape all dressed up in the glamour of something more.

His hair was thinning on the top and his muttonchop sideburns seemed to have thickened to make up for it, like the hair hadn't gone, just migrated down to the sides. Like gravity was winning its battle against him. They hung dense on either side of his rounded face, slimming it to something almost handsome when he was seen head on. When he was staring at himself in the mirror, he looked the best that he ever had, but seen from the sides he had a comically archaic look, like he was some old colonial mayor—someone of station and power, no matter which bit of history he got dropped into. If he'd been handsome, or less funny looking in all his forced grandeur, then he wouldn't have been so easy to like, or to trust. But with all of these funny affectations he verged on being a clown. A caricature of the successful businessman. A cartoon character and, as such, completely harmless.

Victor saw all of that. He took it in, and he smiled at his latest customer. There was money here; every inch of the image that Clifford projected hinted at it. As he rattled off his extravagant order, it was all that Victor could do to keep up. Letterheads, holographic business cards, envelopes, gold leaf on everything. Everything—money was no object. He had two busy businesses both booming and he needed the world to know what a success he was. He didn't say it in so many words, but he screamed it in everything that he did. With the massive order placed and the back of the print shop already rolling into action to accommodate it, this living embodiment of the American dream reached into his back pocket and pulled out his wallet. It was thick to the point of bursting. Hundred-dollar notes squeezed in so tight that they were crumpled at the edges.

Victor's eyes widened as Clifford gestured with the wallet, like it weighed nothing, like it wasn't more money than this shop turned over in a month. Did they want a deposit or did they trust him?

For the very first time, there was an edge to the conversation, and Victor felt like he might be getting a glimpse of how this bumbling joke of a man made his money: the silence that he left, and refused to fill, the sudden tension that came with just a cock of his head. This was definitely a man who could cut a deal. A man who could turn up the pressure. The silence only stretched for a moment before Victor couldn't take any more. No need for a deposit. We're all friends here. And just as though it had never moved an inch, Clifford's smile was back again and he had a fat-fingered hand stretched out to shake. Victor couldn't hesitate now, not with nearly a thousand dollars on the line. He reached out and suffered through the bone grinding shake that followed. It wasn't like there was malice in Clifford's beady little eyes, just the need to show he was the boss. The biggest dog in the park. Victor made sure to keep a straight face even as his hand began to pound in rhythm to his heartbeat. Showing weakness in front of a guy like this cost you respect, and respect was return business with a different hat on. Seemingly satisfied, Clifford released Victor's hand and headed for the door. He was heading to the next town over; he'd come to settle up and get his stationery later. All good. No complaints. Everyone was satisfied. Through the plate glass of the front window, Victor watched him go, the cloud of blue smoke thinning as the moments ticked by, the glamour that the man had projected fading just as fast. Why hadn't he taken a deposit? Why hadn't he had the guy pay upfront? It was so much money, so much stock that would be ruined if the guy didn't come back. It had all happened like a dream, reality only creeping in from the edges now that Clifford was gone. He couldn't be sure anything had happened at all. There was nothing signed, nothing but the ache in his hand and his own scribbled notes of the order to prove Clifford had ever been there at all. Could it have all been a daydream on a dull afternoon? Clifford had certainly seemed like an imaginary character.

That was when the sun glinted off the hologram on the business card still resting on the countertop. The example that Clifford had given of exactly what he wanted. Victor lifted it up to eye level with a sigh, then he got to work.

Out on the street, Clifford rolled on, lighting a new fat stogie cigar from the last one, then pausing in his strut to twist the ball of his foot on the remains of the last one. The sun was shining, the sky was blue. It could not be a better day.

At the end of the street there was a little mom and pop grocery store, and he stepped inside to pick himself up a soda, not even pausing in his stride when he caught the tail end of an argument between the shopkeeper and some teenager. Nothing could slow his stride. Nothing could take the spring from his step. Outside, he rested a shoulder on the side of the building and took a long draw on the bottle. Life just couldn't get better than this. It really couldn't.

The teenager came out looking dejected, all fight gone out of him now. Not even noticing Clifford in his cloud, he trudged off up the road, still grumbling and muttering to himself.

'They weren't hiring?'

The boy hadn't even noticed the colourful mass of Clifford falling into step beside him. Despite his girth, it was like his footsteps made no sound. Like he was a big cat. He was certainly smiling like the cat that got the cream. 'They said I'm too young.'

'Bullshit.' Clifford said it so casually that the boy actually did a double-take. He'd never heard an adult talking like that. Certainly not to a stranger. 'You look big enough to be working to me. How old are you?'

There was a momentary pause as the boy made some internal calculations, trying to work out where this was going, what he could get out of it. Clifford bobbed along beside him as if he didn't care whether he got his answer or not. Finally, the kid let out a sigh. 'Fifteen.'

'Fifteen? I was working building sites when I was fourteen. What a crock! Can't work in a shop but you can carry brick?' He shook his head in disgust, then just went on strolling along in companionable silence while the kid was left holding the figurative ball.

The longer it went with Clifford strolling alongside him, saying nothing at all, stretching out the awkward silence, the more desperately the boy felt like he had to say something, until finally, he blurted out, 'I could carry bricks.'

Clifford smiled to himself then slipped back into the conversation as though they hadn't missed a step. 'I bet you could, strong lad like you.'

There was an edge of heckling in that. The hint of sarcasm lurking just below the surface of the conversation. It made the already riled up boy raise his voice. 'I'm strong enough to do construction!'

Chomping down to keep his stogie in place, Clifford threw his arms up in the air. 'Course you are, kid. Look at you. Little Hercules, ain't you?'

The boy was not a little Hercules. He had thin arms and the build of somebody who had not been getting three square meals a day for most of their life. This was not a track and field star, nor was he built like an American football player, the way that Clifford himself still was beneath the upper layer of expensive clothes and the blubber of rich living. There was that persistent edge of mockery. The boy had tried to keep his head down and just walk home, but this jackass was going to keep taking digs at him. He stopped dead and faced the guy.

'What's your problem, man?'

Clifford burst out laughing. 'My problem? I'll tell you...' From the inner pocket of his jacket, he drew out another one of those gold-trimmed business cards with the holographic logo. This one was branded for a completely different company than the one he'd left behind in the print shop, but the business he was in remained clear. Construction. The kid stared down at this gaudy little testament to Clifford's lack of taste with his mouth hanging open. He'd never seen a business card before, let alone held one that felt so expensive. Thick, creamy card brushed over his fingertips as Clifford plucked it back from his grasp. 'My problem is that I hired a kid to work a site up on Whistler Mountain and he didn't show up today. Didn't call in sick, didn't book a holiday, nothing. Just a no show. And I still need to keep things turning over. You don't get big gigs like this every day. You need to keep the client happy, you know?'

The kid nodded his head as if he had the first inkling of what Clifford was talking about. 'So, what do you say kid? Want to make some money?'

It was only then that it finally clicked into place in the boy's mind. 'You're offering me a job?'

'No. I'm offering you the chance to earn one. You come up to the site, I put you through your paces, see if you're up to the work. It turns out you can cut it, you've got a job for the summer, or a permanent spot on one of my crews if you ain't got school to be going back to. If I take you up there and you can't do a damn thing right, knock stuff over, don't bother turning up one morning, then you'll be out on your ass faster than you can spell your own name. So, what do you say?'

That awkward silence slammed back into place, but the boy knew without a doubt what he needed to do. There was no turning down an offer this good. He held out his hand. 'Sounds like you've got yourself a deal, mister.'

When Clifford took the kid's hand and shook it, there was no pressure. It was almost a caress over the boy's uncalloused palm rather than a real shake.

They headed off to Clifford's car so that he could drive the kid off up into the mountains. Companionable chit chat followed them all the way until they were out of town and up to speed.

Once civilisation had slipped out of sight in the rear-view mirror, the older man fell dead silent. The kid tried to keep up both ends of the conversation, but before long he gave up. He kept looking Clifford's way, and for the life of him, he could not see the amiable businessman who'd come ambling along and offered him a solution to all of his problems. His stare was blank, his eyes dark and distant, even the perpetual smirk that the stogie in the corner of his mouth forced on his ruddy face looked more like a rictus of hate than a smile now. He turned to look at the boy, and for a moment the kid saw the darkness behind his eyes and it stole his breath.

There was just something about Clifford.

No Silver Spoon

On the first day of 1940, Clifford and Leona Olson had their firstborn son. There was all the usual rejoicing in St Paul's Hospital at the happy occasion, but there was also a tinge of disappointment throughout the proceedings. The labour had been long, and the boy hadn't come out until after ten o'clock in the evening. The big prizes for the first children born in the new decade had already been handed out. There was no silver spoon or case of canned milk for little Clifford Junior. All that he got was a baby book from Cunningham's Drug Store and his name in the local paper. Hardly the fame and fanfare that he would later feel like he deserved.

The family returned to their home by the Pacific National Exhibition Grounds in Vancouver the same day, with the squalling little boy wrapped up in blankets that they'd had to pay for themselves instead of being gifted like some of those other children. The house was small, big enough for the three of them, certainly, but not for the three other children that soon followed him into life. Two brothers, Richard and Dennis, and a sister, Sharon, appeared in the house over the next five years.

Leona was a dedicated homemaker, doing what she could to make their meagre income stretch to hearty meals and hard-wearing clothes. Hand-me-downs were darned as the children outgrew them, ready for the next baby to grow into them. Despite this, they did not live in squalor, nor did they ever know much in the way of real strife.

Clifford Senior worked as a milkman in the early years, driving one of the last horse-drawn carts to deliver milk to every house in the early hours of the morning. As time rolled on he began taking on extra jobs here and there, until eventually the little jobs he was doing transformed into a new career as he was employed full-time as a labourer for a local builder.

The almost idyllic suburban existence was rocked by events on the world stage. The Second World War had broken out in Europe and it changed everything. Unlike their southern neighbours, Canada did not attempt a platform of non-involvement when evil was being done on a grand scale. They were still a part of the commonwealth, and they meant to aid Great Britain in their war against the Axis powers in whatever manner they could. At first, there was only material support being offered, but it was not long before they were drawn into the conflict directly after only a brief period of their shipping lanes coming under attack from German U-boats.

Being a man of principle, Clifford Senior signed up. He could not look himself in the eye if he knew that his fellow Canadians were dying in the mud of France while he stayed behind, moving bricks around when he could have been there, doing the right thing and making the world a better place for his children.

When he could come home, he did, to the immense delight of his family, but those visits were few and far between, and each time he seemed a little smaller, a little more diminished. He was a giant of a man in the eyes of his children, but each time he came home he was a little quieter, a little softer with them. By the time that the war was over, his voice had gone from a booming voice heard all through the house to a soft whisper heard only when they were being held close, a vibration that spread down through his arms and chest to surround them. All the bluster he'd carried before was gone. All that he wanted now was for his family to be safe and happy.

When the war was over, things changed again, but this time for the better. There was an extensive program in Canada to provide mortgages and housing to veterans, and the Olson family took up every offer that they were given, relocating from the relative isolation of their old home to the brand new, soon to be bustling metropolis of Richmond.

Whole swathes of the town were being built from the ground up to offer housing to all of the veterans taking the government up on their version of the GI Bill, and while Clifford Senior was quick to take one of the early houses on Gilmore Crescent, he was also delighted to discover that there was more work than he could ever need in the construction business. So many skilled men had been lost in the war that anyone with any sort of experience in the industry was now finding themselves in high demand and receiving much more reasonable pay as a result. They moved into one of those freshly built houses, which was frankly palatial compared to their old home, and settled into what should have been a comfortable middle class existence.

Clifford Junior had reached the grand old age of five by the time that they moved into their new home, and just as the new school was finished being built, it was his time to start attending. At five, he was short, stocky, and poorly socialized in comparison to all of his peers. Most of them had lived in British Columbia for their whole lives, many of them sharing nursery schools or at least local parks. They were all known to each other, and Clifford Junior was a stranger.

He took the initial distance between him and the other students as a rejection. A rejection that he'd never forgive for the rest of his life. His foul mood followed him home, upsetting his brothers and sisters. There was no outlet for his frustration, and he certainly didn't have enough emotional maturity to discuss the matter with his family, or to work through his feelings himself.

At school, after less than a week, he picked his first fight. Even at home, he was stubborn, rude, and unwilling to show weakness in front of anyone. It was the perfect storm to turn a mildly ostracized boy into the enemy of the whole school year. The only trouble was, young Clifford wasn't any more competent with his fists than anything else relating to school. He lost every one of the fights that he started, and it soon became a running joke that he was the class punching bag. Still, he wouldn't relent or change his behaviour in any way. He was in the right, they were in the wrong, and some day he was going to prove to every single one of them that just because they'd won the fights, it didn't mean that they were going to win the war.

As the years rolled on, his reputation never changed. He struggled with his studies, scraping through with the lowest grades that allowed him to continue advancing through school with the rest of the class. Even when given the resources and assistance that he really needed to do better, he'd reject them or ignore them, as if he could brute force his own way through school the same way he'd failed to brute force his way through a social life. His attention never seemed to focus on the work, even when he claimed that he was trying his hardest. He just couldn't seem to bring himself to care enough to do more than the bare minimum. It didn't help that all of his brothers were now attending the same school and excelling, marking him even more clearly as the worthless black sheep of the family.

He came home every day with fresh bruises. With letters warning he was on the verge of failure. With new tears in his clothes that his mother had to stitch up while his father looked on in silence. Did that silence hold the disdain that the younger Clifford thought it did? Or had the war hollowed him out, leaving nothing inside?

Clifford Senior was no longer frantically labouring to make ends meet. With the completion of construction on the town, he had moved into property management and maintenance instead. He was the super for local apartment buildings and a few of the surrounding homes, a well-known and respected member of the community, with more free time than he knew what to do with, for the first time in his life.

He chose to spend that time with his children and helping out around the house instead of drinking or gambling like so many of his peers. He took the kids down to the local park, to concerts, to anything that might spark some joy in them, setting aside time for each one of them to get his personal attention. The younger children thrived under that attention, learning new skills from their father, embracing shared interests and hobbies, and becoming closer to their family while also growing into the people that they would one day become.

None of it seemed to work with Clifford Junior. He remained sullen and spiteful despite all of his father's attempts to connect with him. He trudged through the events that all the other kids took joy in, and he sapped any enjoyment that his father might have found in them, too. That is until, one day, an exhibition boxing match was in town, and Clifford Senior smuggled his eldest in to see the match even though he knew that Leona would not have approved of such a thing.

For the first time, he saw the boy's eyes light up. He saw excitement and joy play out over the kid's face as the rhythmic thump of fist on flesh echoed out through the dimly lit hall. When blood was spilt, Cliff Junior was up on his feet, screaming and baying like the rest of the crowd. Enraptured. Clifford Senior barely even saw the bout itself, eyes locked on his son as he came alive.

For days afterwards, boxing was all that little Cliff would talk about until, finally, once again unbeknownst to his mother, Clifford Senior took him to a gym in the middle of town. It was an old-fashioned place with sawdust on the floor and the reek of sweat permeating every part of it. The leather punching bags creaked as they swung from exposed rafters, and all the soldiers who hadn't been able to let go of the aggression that the war put in them came to let it all out. Cliff was booked in for boxing lessons, and while his father couldn't come and watch the boy each time without embarrassing him, there was no small measure of pride in him when he picked the boy up to walk him home and he was regaled with stories. Young Cliff's face was flushed, taking on the same ruddiness as his father's when he was excited, and his eyes shone in the streetlights.

Before long there was talk of entering him into competitions. Clifford Senior was invited in to talk it over, and he marvelled as his clumsy, chubby lump of a son danced on the balls of his feet within the ring. Ducking and diving punches that could have floored a grown man and striking back with enough power to stagger even the biggest opponents. He was in his element on the canvas. An artist with his gloves. Clifford Senior couldn't look away, even when the boy's practice bout was over and he got set to work on one of the heavy bags. Where was this boy when they were outside of the gym? Where was all this energy and excitement and flair? It was like he was looking at somebody else's son.

There was talk of him becoming a real contender, maybe stepping out for America at the Olympics in a few years' time once he was in his prime. They talked about diet and exercise and trying him out in a few amateur matches against other boxing clubs to see how he did. There was a bright and promising future for a talented boxer in those days. The sport was at the height of its popularity.

Meanwhile, Clifford Junior was making his own plans for the future—plans that did not involve his day in the limelight but certainly revolved around his newfound ability to beat any man he met in a fistfight.

Throughout his educational career, almost every boy in his class had made a fool of him and beaten him down when he objected. Most of the other boys in the school, too, had taken their turn at using him as a punching bag. He had never backed down from a fight, even though he had lost them all, and the list of boys who had knocked him around had crept from dozens to over a hundred.

This list was not figurative. Clifford Junior could recite their names, if prompted, and starting with the very first boy to ever throw a punch his way, he began to work through that list. One by one, he visited the boys where they were playing outside their homes, and he demonstrated his new skills as a boxer. None of these children were prepared for a trained combatant to unleash his fury on them. This time around they lost. One by one, they lost. And with every one that fell, Clifford Junior felt better about himself. He took great pride in seeing his one-time bullies flinching away from him and an even more profound joy in the fact that all those who had struck him in the past were now quaking in fear, just waiting for his inevitable vengeance to rain down upon them.

His reputation in school transformed as his prowess became more widely known. He became a source of fear for the other children rather than a source of mirth. If there was ever trouble brewing, you could be certain that Clifford was at the heart of it, and if he had the opportunity to instigate conflict, he inevitably would. He went from being too shy to talk in class to arguing openly with his teachers if he disagreed with their lessons. Like so many uneducated people, he was under the mistaken impression that his opinion held as much weight as those who held expertise, and he was damned if he was going to let anyone talk down to him ever again. He went from being unpopular and rejected to being loathed but respected by his peers. A social life of sycophants began to develop around him, and gradually he was drawn into the periphery of the normal social life of the school through them—and through the fear of reprisal if he was not invited along to events.

With his goals achieved, his interest in boxing began to dwindle. He could already out-fight everyone that he met. Why did he need to train harder so he could beat people he'd never even cross paths with? He didn't need to be the toughest guy in the world, just here. He delighted in being the big fish in the small pond. A classic small-town bully.

He would still show up for the fun parts of boxing, when there were matches scheduled for him to participate in or other contenders to spar with, but the day-to-day training required to keep him in condition was no longer entertaining enough to hold his interest without the prize at the end of the rainbow. As he refused to train properly, more and more opportunities that had once been extended to him faded away until the parts of the sport that he had truly delighted in were no longer available to him. Another chip on his shoulder, another awful slight that was caused by his own behaviour rather than some grand conspiracy against him.

It mattered very little, because at about this point in his life, Clifford's hormones had kicked in, and suddenly his interest in anything other than sex rapidly dropped off. While he'd learned early that women were impressed by his feats of violence, he'd also learned just as quickly that he had nothing more to offer them. He was not conventionally attractive at that age, and even with his musculature, it wasn't enough to maintain any sort of relationship for longer than a conversation.

Still, he was spending more and more time out with his so-called friends, most of whom only wanted to be associated with him so that they felt safe from any threats of violence. They were the scum that rose to the top of his school cohort and their wider social circle, and they were all on course to long criminal careers. For the most part, their crimes were more white-collar than he might have managed for himself. There were pimps, con-artists, and tricksters aplenty, and soon Clifford began to find his own voice—and his own gift for talking.

Before, Clifford had always felt awkward or uncomfortable, but he noticed his new friends could shrug off any number of rejections and rebuffs without so much as flinching, much the same way he was able to power through the punches of his opponents in the ring. Once the fear was gone, he suddenly realised that not only could he talk to anybody, he was good at it. Better than most of the con men even, because they were always too slick. They never let the person they were chatting with see them stumble. They slipped right through trustworthy and out the other side by projecting an image of themselves that was too perfect. Clifford didn't do any of that. Not because he wasn't smart enough or capable enough, as his old schoolmates might have suggested, but because he was making a calculated choice to show weakness and failure, to make himself the butt of a joke and laugh along with it. It should have required immense maturity to deliberately place himself in emotional harm's way like that, but nothing could be further from the truth. Clifford could not be hurt by the words of others because he didn't consider them to be fully human, or real. Their opinion of him didn't matter because by the time the conversation was over and he'd gotten what he wanted from them, he'd never see them again. They were pieces in a game, not real people, and that meant he didn't have to feel anything about lying to them, making a fool of himself, or anything else. Nothing mattered, so he could do anything he felt like.

His skill with his tongue rapidly surpassed his skill with his fists, but his reputation for being the worst kind of bully never faded. He rarely resorted to violence now that he had a much easier alternative, but instead of strolling up to a kid and demanding their lunch money under threat of violence, he now tricked them out of it, and he considered every act of fraud and trickery to be intensely amusing. The world had looked at him and considered him stupid, and now he was tricking them all every single day. That was a bigger rush than beating on the boys who had once overpowered him. He wasn't just getting the best of one kid; he was getting the best of everybody. He was better than everybody, and now he could prove it, day after day.

With the combination of skills that he had developed by the age of sixteen, Clifford no longer felt any real compulsion to go on attending school. He hadn't learned anything there since the first day on the playground when some bigger kid cracked his teeth. The strong prey on the weak. Lesson learned.

His attendance had already been spotty since the age of 10, so having him gradually show up for fewer and fewer classes didn't really sound any alarm bells, and when he officially left Cambie Junior High School in 1956, there was a fair amount of silent rejoicing from the teachers who had suffered through his constant attitude problems since he'd first started attending their school.

Of course, his parents wouldn't have allowed him to simply step out of education and into the criminal underworld he seemed destined for. Yet both of them found Clifford Junior to be a changed person, too. The sullen boy they'd known all his life was gone, replaced by a charming young man who could convince them quite easily that nothing had gone awry with his life. He wasn't built for academia, and he'd rather start supporting the family now than dawdling on for a few more years and coming away with no qualifications to speak of. He made a compelling case, even if it was founded almost entirely on false promises. So they consented to let him leave school on the condition that he found himself a job first.

For the fast-talking teen, it was barely even an effort. He strolled into his new job at the Old Lansdown racetrack on the same day his parents made their demand, and he immediately began excelling. Officially, his job was simply to take bets from the patrons, but it wasn't long before he was manipulating the odds by dropping entirely fabricated hints about the predicted outcomes of races to the punters. From there it was a short distance to taking his own bets on the side and fudging records to cover any losses. If his employers ever became aware of his scam artistry, they must have turned a blind eye to it thanks to the sheer amount of money he made for them. Besides, if any customer ever became angry enough to take matters into their own hands, they were confronted with a man who could still quite easily have been a professional boxer if he so chose. A man that it suddenly seemed unwise to cross.

Clifford got a taste of money for the first time in his life. He realised that his wicked little games of extortion and trickery weren't just entertaining, but profitable, too. Once again, it felt like all the pieces were finally coming together for him, all of the disparate parts of his life drawing together to show him his course forward.

Of course, Clifford was not satisfied with the meagre amount that he made bilking unfortunates at the track. He knew that there was more money out there for a man with his talents. He could go anywhere and do anything with his gift for deception and trickery, so why shouldn't he?

The first place that he went was back to the drunks and scum he'd been associating with in the first place. None of them ever struggled for cash, and none of them ever seemed to put in a day's work. Better yet, most of them trusted him implicitly, still looking on him as a naive child. They were his contacts with the criminal underworld of this new town, and he was going to use them for all that they were worth.

Almost immediately they put him to work. At first, he was little more than a lookout or some hired muscle for small operations, but it wasn't long before he graduated to taking on whole criminal enterprises for himself. He'd work his day at the track, swing by a bar in the evening to pick up some juicy leads, and then get to work on what he increasingly considered to be his real job. More often than not that just involved rolling drunks for their wallets, sometimes a little more aggressive mugging. He smoothed things over with his charm as much as possible, made it seem like he was on the victim's side against the other roughs that were gathered in the shadows. Made it seem like giving him their wallet was the easy way out, a way for them to walk away unscathed from the animals that this nice young man was trying to fend off. It was such a successful routine that he never even got reported to the police.

From there it was a natural graduation to learning the time-honoured art of burglary from some of the worst locals that Richmond had to offer. They were truly terrible at their craft, and it didn't take long before Cliff had not only learned everything that they had to teach but also surpassed them in every way. He had a level of athleticism and cold calculation that the vast majority of the addicts and criminals were lacking, and he put it to work, keeping track of who had the most cash to throw around at his day job and then tracking the wealthiest of them home so that he could mark their houses for late night explorations. It worked perfectly for months—too well, in fact. He was hitting so many homes of so many wealthy people that the police began to suspect that organised crime was behind it. While there was no real pattern to the neighbourhoods that Clifford was targeting, it was easy enough for the police to narrow down their patrols to the few streets in Richmond where there were potential targets that had not been hit recently. His own surprising precision and planning ended up being his undoing. If he had been clumsy, re-treading the same ground like most of his older counterparts, then he would never have been picked up. As it was, a patrol car spotted him climbing in through a window and he was caught in the act of burglary.

His family were mortified to discover that they had a criminal living under their roof. His father, already a quiet man, refused to speak to him at all. Only his mother served as a bridge of communication to him while he was in jail awaiting trial. Everything that they could do to protect him from the consequences of his actions, they did, even though it brought them immeasurable shame.

Though it cost them their savings, the family managed to procure a lawyer for Clifford Junior who would help him avoid a serious prison sentence. The argument that they presented was that he was still a child in the eyes of the law and should be treated as such. While the local police were certainly pushing for Clifford to be tried as an adult given the extent of his crimes, there was no evidence that he had been involved in any burglary beyond the one that he was caught in the middle of. Everything that he'd taken in the past months, he'd passed off directly to a fence without delay. All that the police had found when they searched the Olson house was an ample hoard of untraceable cash.

The judge was convinced to uphold the usual letter of the law, but he insisted on a custodial sentence all the same, to scare some sense into Clifford Junior and put him back on the straight and narrow. He was committed into the care of the New Haven Borstal Correctional Centre in Burnaby. He was to serve out nine months, until his 18th birthday, when he would be released on his own recognisance. Probably the most sensible course, since it seemed that his family could no longer bear to even look at him after what he had done and what he had put them all through.

New Haven was not the ideal situation for Clifford. All of the things that he had hated about school were amplified tenfold in a borstal. Every moment of his life was dictated to him by guards and teachers. Every moment of free time that he had to relax, he was being watched constantly to make sure that he didn't step out of line. It could have been enough to do exactly what the judge had wanted and scared him straight, but that would have required a level of introspection that was beyond Clifford at that age. All that he felt was hatred and rage towards the people that had put him in this position. But of course, his present circumstances prevented him from seeking out any vengeance. The one good thing that had carried over from his school career, at least from his perspective, was his reputation as the toughest guy around. This was a prison for children, and here he was, a hulking man before his time, more than ready and willing to lash out at the slightest provocation. He was every bit the bully he had always been now that he was forced back into the same circumstances. His silver tongue turned caustic and his knuckles were bloodied more days than not.

The only benefit that Clifford drew from his time in the borstal was the recognition that there were other pleasures he could take from his victims beyond simply humiliating them. It did not take long before he witnessed his first homosexual rape in the all-boys school, and it took even less time afterwards for him to begin perpetrating the same grotesque violence on others. As a seventeen-year-old at the top of the pecking order, Clifford Junior was offered up the cream of the crop. The most feminine-looking boys in the borstal were set aside for his use, and his reputation protected them from the predations of lesser rapists—though in his stereotypical, uncaring way, he quite frequently allowed others in his clique to violate them all the same.

It is safe to say that there was nobody in New Haven that was more hated than Clifford Olson Junior. So, it should come as no surprise that everyone, both inmates and staff, breathed a sigh of relief when he made his escape.

There was no cunning plan, carefully prepared tunnel, or outsmarting of the guards. There was simply an athletic young man who knew that the best way out of his current situation was to run like hell. The walls were not high enough, and the trees growing nearby had been allowed to reach a height that they should not have. From there, Clifford took off on foot through the woods, following alongside the road and heading home to Richmond before anyone back in the prison was even certain that he'd escaped to begin with. Once the alarm was raised, the first place that the police were sent was his family home, but the other Olsons had no idea that the black sheep of their clan was heading in their direction.

Still, Cliff Junior was no fool. He knew that Richmond was the first place that they would come looking for him now that he'd made his escape, and he didn't intend to be there when they came looking. Using his old stomping ground as familiar territory to launch the next stage of his escape, he made it down to the waterfront and stole a speedboat with which he meant to put some distance between him and the prison. If he could cross state lines, then it was likely that the resultant bureaucracy would protect him from any consequences long enough to secure some new criminal contacts, some wealth, and move along to some new, even more distant bolt hole.

It seemed that this was not to be, however. For all of his skills, Clifford could not sweet talk or brutalise a speed boat into going where he wanted it to go when he had no training. The police were almost upon him before he even made it clear of the dock, and from there it was a simple matter of taking to the river in speedboats of their own and keeping up the pressure. To his credit, he gave the police a run for their money, swerving his way up-river at as close to full speed as he could coax out of his little boat, but struggling badly to avoid the simple obstacles that any seasoned sailor could have spotted from miles off. Unfortunately for him, a good portion of the local police department owned boats of their own. They may not have been able to keep up with his insane recklessness, but they were more than capable of making up the distance as Clifford bounced off logs or scraped over sandbanks. As they rounded another bend, with Clifford barely maintaining control of his ship, they were finally close enough to bring him to a halt.

A single warning shot was fired off the prow of his ship, throwing up a spray of water to spritz him in the face. He was no fool— despite what his elementary teachers and parents might have thought. He knocked the motor out of gear, stood up and held his hands in the air as the engine roared and stalled.

The pursuing cops circled his boat, yelling commands, and he just didn't seem to care. He stood there, grinning to himself in the winter's breeze as they dragged his ship to the shore, boarded, and arrested him.

He had immediately surrendered the moment that his life was in danger, knowing perfectly well that this was just going to be the first of many opportunities to get himself free of the criminal justice system.

As he was manhandled off of his stolen boat and into custody, with heavy chains linking up his wrists and ankles, he laughed out loud, claiming to the cops that picked him up that he didn't care. All of this had been for nothing, and they had wasted their whole night chasing after a free man. When his birthday came along in a few weeks' time he'd be back out on the streets anyway. There was nothing that anybody could do to stop him.

The court disagreed with that sentiment, as it turned out. For his breakout attempt, two years were added to his custodial sentence, time to be served without any chance of parole. He stood unflinching in the stand as the sentence was passed down, the same smug smirk on his face. He'd already broken out once—how hard would it be to take another walk after they'd marched him back to borstal?

Unfortunately for him, the judge had also taken the ease of his escape into account during sentencing, and since it seemed that a mere borstal could not hold him, the judge finally enacted the punishment that the police had been demanding for him from the outset. He would be sent to an adult prison, to serve out the remainder of his time doing hard labour rather than lounging around in classes that he took no interest in. He would no longer be the biggest fish in a small pond. He would be a big fish in a tank full of sharks.

The Purchase of Freedom

Haney Correctional Facility was the first of many prisons that Clifford Junior would spend time in. It was a dour and oppressive place, a world away from the relative peace of the borstal where he'd previously been contained. There was no more easy prey for him stalking the halls, and he learned swiftly that the things that had gained him respect in his old facility now made the other prisoners look on him with contempt. He was no longer the big guy picking on the runts of the litter. He was a child in a man's world. Despite his youth, Cliff's sophomoric attempts to establish his presence at least gave the rest of the prison a solid enough impression of him as a fighter that he wasn't preyed upon in turn, but he was nowhere near running the place like he'd been in New Haven.

With no real place in the hierarchy, he was left mostly to his own devices. He managed a few rape attempts against weaker inmates who were similarly abandoned in the system, but he never had the lasting power required to gain any sort of monopoly on them. To make matters worse, he constantly found his movements curtailed by the guards, who had him marked as a troublemaker after his previous escape attempt. There was meant to be a strict and ordered regimen that every prisoner in

Haney followed, but for the most part, it was not directly enforced. Meals were scheduled at certain times, of course, as was exercise time in the yard, but beyond that, if prisoners did not have a work detail, they were essentially free to entertain themselves. Not so for Clifford. He was confined to his cell as much as was possible, and when he wasn't, he could constantly feel the eyes of guards on him. He rebelled, fighting back against them when they tried to force him into routines, resulting in even worse treatment and black marks on his record that eventually could have led to his sentence being lengthened.

Still, the guards weren't entirely stupid. On the days when they were short-staffed or simply distracted with other duties, they found that Clifford was actually quite good at following the prescribed routines. His only issue with the schedule seemed to be that they were forcing him to follow it. The problem was with authority being exerted over him, not with what was being asked of him. When the guards backed off, they soon discovered that Clifford was a compliant prisoner.

Accordingly, he earned a little bit of respect and relief from the guards. It was clear to him that he wasn't going to be making any progress climbing the ladder of society within prison, given the prolific career criminals he would have to surpass, so he turned to the only other possible path to improve his stay. He started informing on his fellow inmates.

With his smooth talking, it was simple enough for him to learn about all of the comings and goings of his fellow prisoners. Initially, he had ingratiated himself with them, thinking that there might be ongoing escape attempts that he could latch onto to win his freedom, but when that proved fruitless, he began learning as much as possible about every ongoing or past criminal enterprise in action within the prison so that he could drip feed information out to the guards in exchange for preferential treatment. Any extra time that they might have requested for him was burned away by their gratitude, and the two years that he had initially been scheduled to serve within the prison started to be eaten away at, too.

Had the other prisoners ever learned that he was behind the successive crackdowns on smuggling rings and drug dealing behind bars, it's likely that Clifford would have been on the receiving end of one of the makeshift weapons that he eventually ended up warning the guards were hidden around the place, but his luck held throughout the remainder of his sentence. Within a little over a year, his time in Haney was over, and he was released back onto the streets, completely unchanged by his time in prison.

From the moment that he was back on the streets, he was back to his old tricks. With little else to do in prison, he had gotten himself into fighting shape again, and so his late-night muggings no longer required the participation of any accomplices. Many of his old contacts in the criminal underworld had dried up, with the majority serving prison sentences even longer than his, and whatever money he had been waiting to receive from his fence was long gone, along with all traces of them. His family took him back in, despite knowing better, giving him a roof over his head and clothes to wear, but they never took him entirely into their trust again, and after a short while living in limbo with them, Clifford Junior decided that it was time to move on.

Despite having nothing tying him to his hometown, Clifford still couldn't move freely throughout the country due to his probationary conditions. He may no longer have been in prison, but the judicial system still had a claw in him. He was not allowed to leave the province of British Columbia, and he had to report any change of address to the police immediately or he'd face imprisonment all over again. In the end, he had only barely made it to nearby New Westminster and reported his new address in a flophouse before the police came and picked him up as a suspect for some neighbourhood burglaries which had, by sheer coincidence, began at almost the same exact time as his arrival in town. He did not have the established network of contacts required in this new town to move things along, and it didn't take long before a local pawn shop identified some of the items he'd delivered to them as stolen and passed the information along to the police. He had been out only a matter of weeks before he found himself back in jail awaiting trial all over again.

This time there was no question of youthful hijinks or being led astray, and the court-issued lawyer was in no way motivated to try and keep what he viewed as a career criminal out on the streets. Due diligence was done, minimal sentencing was requested, but the case was open and shut, and Clifford had no leverage. His new sentence was considerably longer than the last. When combined with the time that he had not served for his previous escape attempt, it brought the term up to almost a decade.

His latest sentence was to be served at the British Columbia Penitentiary, a maximum-security prison that made his previous incarcerations seem positively pleasant by comparison. Built in 1878, it was more of a castle than a prison, a huge looming stone building that was home to more than a little dark history. While the place had been an impenetrable fortress for most of its history, time was beginning to wear on it, and in the 30s, riots had broken out that swept through the whole structure, eventually leading to the Canadian government reforming the treatment of prisoners so that any labour while within prison was compensated. Admittedly, they were only paid five cents a day, but it was markedly better than the nothing that they had received previously. Regardless, it seemed that the place was perpetually on the verge of violence and chaos, holding some of the most dangerous prisoners in Canada. The level of brutality that the guards and inmates inflicted upon each other was escalating by the time that Clifford was incarcerated there, and he stepped into a powder-keg.

Placed in a cell with a serial rapist, Gary Marcoux, Cliff was expected to serve as a punching bag, or worse—something to contain his cell-mate's unchecked sexual aggression towards the other prisoners. Instead, he befriended the man, using his smooth talking to get into the other man's good books, playing the naïve new guy who wanted to learn the ropes, and gradually building up trust until finally, he managed to extract a confession from the man about the rape and murder of a little girl that the police hadn't managed to pin on him. It was the kind of information that might earn the right person a good few years shaved off their sentence.

He made contact with the guards and was ushered into the warden's office, where he disclosed all he had learned and was met with blank-faced denial. Unless he had some evidence to go with his fanciful tale, there was nothing on the table for him. If, on the other hand, he somehow secured something that would be admissible in court as something other than hearsay, then they could talk about time off for good behaviour. Clifford left the office, fuming at having been so thoroughly ignored, but he did not abandon his plan so easily. He'd managed to manipulate Gary into spilling his deepest darkest secrets—how hard would it be to get him to give up the rest?

What followed was a complex game of cat and mouse as Cliff did everything in his power to keep himself in Gary's good graces whilst also applying pressure to him to give up something that he might use to ruin the man's life further. In the end, the solution came not from Gary himself, but from some of the other criminal activities that the diligent and devoted rat came upon. Illegal liquor was being brewed in the bathrooms, and in exchange for a few favours, Cliff managed to acquire some of the rancid smelling liquid for himself. After lockdown at night, when such contraband would usually be consumed in private, he did the unthinkable and offered to share it with his cellmate.

What followed was a long night of drinking and soft chatter. Gary didn't realise how little of the noxious brown swill Cliff was actually consuming, and he certainly didn't realise what was happening when the pen was pushed into his hand and Cliff took up a position behind him, massaging his shoulders and coaching him through writing out his confession and signing it.

When he awoke the next morning with a burning hangover and the taste of death in his mouth, Gary rose to his feet, fully expecting to find Cliff in a similar state in his bunk. He was nowhere to be seen. Still fuzzy on the events of the previous night, Gary meandered over to the toilet, did his business and was on his way back to the bunk for a much-needed lie down again when memory struck him like a hammer blow. The letter. The confession. Where had he put it? He tore their room apart, but there was no sign of the paper towel that he had used to seal his fate. Clifford. That little rat had tricked him into this. He was going to find him, take the paper back, rip it into shreds, flush it, and then he was going to murder that little bastard for putting him through all this. He was going to choke the life out of him, if he could stretch his fingers around the kid's thick neck.

He took off at a run throughout the prison, searching all the little rat's usual hiding places, but there was no sign of Clifford anywhere. Asking around the other prisoners turned up nothing either. It wasn't until lunchtime when he finally did the unthinkable and turned to the guards for help, asking where the hell his cellmate had gotten to. These were not people in the know. They just passed along what they had been told. Clifford was in solitary confinement for the foreseeable future.

With his signed confession in hand, the police swung into motion pulling Gary out of the prison and putting him back in front of a judge and jury to face the consequences of his awful crime. Now it was Gary who was kept in silent isolation, away from the rest of the world. Just waiting to stand up and say that it was all a lie, that it was Clifford's invention, that the bastard had made it all up and forged his signature.

Clifford spoke first. While Gary looked every bit the criminal misfit that he'd always been, Clifford had his charm and every appearance of candour on his side. He told the true and factual story of how he'd extracted the confession, even readily admitting to the misdemeanours on his own part that had provided the liquor he'd used to ply the child-killer. It was all entirely true, except for the final words that he spoke, about his conscience not allowing him to sleep in the same room as a man who had committed such awful acts. He didn't care about the little girl, raped and dead, any more than he'd care about a discarded soda bottle—she just happened to provide the thing that he needed.

Gary's attempt to discredit Clifford on the stand all fell flat. Clifford was too good at talking, dissembling, answering questions with questions, twisting things around. Even the lawyers couldn't back him into a corner, and they tried for much longer than you might expect. He was the weak point in the state's case, as far as the defence were concerned. If they could prove he was untrustworthy or a liar, then the confession might be ignored. Proving that a convicted criminal was untrustworthy should not have been difficult. Yet here they were facing his cheerful smile and dullard honesty and finding that all their education could not hold up in the face of his skill with words.

Gary was convicted to a life sentence and transferred to another prison so that Clifford could be safely returned to British Columbia Penitentiary.

Clifford was pleased to find that his remaining sentence had been reduced drastically in thanks for his assistance to the police. He had only two and a half years left to serve after that stunt. For the first few days back in the prison, he was riding a high at having knocked so many years off in a single swing, but soon his treatment by the other prisoners began to turn sour. They spat at him as he walked past their cells, he was pushed and jostled in the dinner line, threats were whispered to him, and rumours were circulated about him. He had openly crossed the line to side with the police against his fellow inmate, and they were not liable to forget that any time soon.

It did not matter that many of them would have proudly boasted about stabbing a child rapist to death in their own right. It was the betrayal of the trust of their peers that was considered to be the great offence, not doing one of them harm. With his being marked as an informer, nobody in the prison would ever trust Clifford again. With increased social isolation, he no longer had his finger on the pulse of the prison's black market and gossip, so the guards lost all use for him, and he lost the kindly treatment that he'd been receiving from them for his services as a rat. He might have had only two and a half years left on his sentence, but they were going to be hard years, not easy ones like he'd enjoyed up until now.

When the constant undercurrent of dissatisfaction in the prison turned into outright chaos, riots, and violence, there was no doubt in his mind that the violence would be directed towards him. He had to get out if he meant to survive.

When the prison's staff were driven out by the inmate uprising, Clifford pursued them, hiding in a closet until the guards had all geared up to go back in and break up the chaos, then slipping out behind them once their battleline had passed him by. Escape was as simple as walking out through the doors that had been left open and then running as fast as his legs would carry him while everyone was distracted.

It would take days before his absence was noted. There were leaders of the rebellion to prosecute and injured guards who needed their wounds tended to. The temporary absence of one minor criminal in the midst of it all didn't need scrutiny. When, days later, it became apparent that Clifford was nowhere on the property, the warden and staff still couldn't believe that he would attempt an escape. There was no logic to the move; he'd cut a ten-year sentence down to practically nothing by comparison. Nobody sane would have tried to break out and risk having all of their original sentence reinstated. It was so ridiculous that the police and prison didn't believe it could be true at first. They'd sooner believe that someone had made some mistake and lost him somewhere in some inmate transfer than believe that he'd made an escape attempt. This dubiousness cost them valuable time before the escape of a prisoner could be announced and a dragnet set up—time that Clifford used to put as much distance as possible between himself and the prison. By the time that checkpoints were established at the maximum range that the police believed a man on foot could travel in the timeframe, Clifford was a block away and still heading out. The dragnet closed seconds behind him, and he walked away a free man.

No Exit

That night, he slept under the Queensborough Bridge in New Westminster, surrounded by the other down and outs of the city, hidden in plain sight but gloating away to himself over his success.

In the days that followed, his escape became front page news in the local newspapers. The police would resort to tracking down Clifford's family and begging them for help in finding him. There was a television appearance by his teary-eyed mother who pleaded for him to turn himself in and save himself from further punishment. There was also an interview with Clifford Olson Senior. 'He knows what he's facing. He might have to serve ten years.' The man had aged drastically since his eldest son had started out on his campaign of crime. 'If he doesn't give himself up, I hope that they get him before he does something really bad. He's done enough bad already.'

It was the last time that his family would publicly acknowledge any connection to him. Needless to say, he did not see the broadcast, nor did he have any intention of going back to jail. In the intervening week, he had stolen several changes of clothes and a backpack, and now he headed off into the wilderness to wait until the hunt for him had cooled down and he might be able to return to some of his old haunts. Apparently, he had underestimated just how furious the police were going to be that he'd slipped by them.

They swept out through the countryside to hunt him, and while he was wily enough to avoid detection by the police, he had more than mere humans to contend with. Rinty the police dog was on the job.

He avoided detection by the hunting policemen by ducking into a copse of blackberry bushes outside of Richmond, slicing himself up on the thorns but considering spilt blood a small price to pay for his ongoing freedom. Once he was thoroughly concealed, he settled in to wait the searchers out. Rinty was not fooled. Sprinting straight into the bundle of blackberries, the dog flung herself bodily into it, crushing Clifford back amidst the tangle of creepers and thorns and thoroughly trapping him as the dog barked her head off, drawing the attention of everyone around her. Eventually, they had to cut Clifford out of the bush, covered in scratches, peppered with embedded thorns, and boasting more than a few bite marks from the excitable pup. Needless to say, he was not amused by the outcome.

Returned to Old BC Penitentiary, Clifford was surprised to find that the court only slapped an additional year onto his sentence after his masterfully executed escape. It seemed that the many reports of good behaviour and compliance throughout the years had weighed rather more heavily on the scales of justice than he would have first anticipated. The guards and warden had taken on the brunt of the blame for his 'moment of madness' in the midst of the riot, but his latest antics had affirmed to the other prisoners that he was as much of a rat as they believed. The constant threat of violence against him continued to mount as stories of his special treatment spread.

Having tried one way of ending his sentence early, Cliff now turned to the other way. It was clear to him that there would be no escaping from the Old BC Penitentiary. The security was just too dense for him to even begin to pick his way around it, especially now that he was considered a flight risk. With one of his shaving razors in hand and his bare wrist exposed, he knew that this was the only way out. The only way to make his torment end. Gritting his teeth, he dug the sharp edge into his flesh.

When the cell doors unlocked in the morning, he was sitting on the side of his bed, not raring to get out of the confines as usual. He called one of the guards in, and they came readily enough, expecting to hear him spinning some new story about another prisoner, hoping for some more table scraps.

Instead, Cliff directed him to the toilet. The bowl was full of unflushed urine, to nobody's surprise given the smell of the room, but there was something darker in it, a slash of red. Blood. The guard gave Clifford a pat on the shoulder and promised him that the prison doctor would be around in the next hour, then they'd get him off to hospital to get whatever it was sorted out. Cliff looked shell-shocked, but he thanked the guard politely all the same. There was no excuse for bad manners, even in a situation like this.

From there, his transfer to the local Shaughnessy Hospital for tests was inevitable, and just as inevitable was that there was practically no security in that hospital, certainly nothing that could compare to the Old BC. While doctors and nurses were treating him like a patient, he was scoping out the place, working out his escape route, gathering intelligence on when the guards watching him changed their shifts and how often they lolled off to sleep on the seat outside his room. All of the due diligence he had never quite learned in his career as a burglar he had now developed after his time in prison. He had honed his observation and timing until he could operate entirely without observation by the authorities. It was a talent that would serve him well in the years to come.

When he was finally left alone, he rose from his bed, stole the clothes of another patient while they were sleeping, changed in the bathroom, and then strolled out of the building, a new man.

Three guards had been sent along with him to ensure that there was no trouble, and the idea that he could have slipped by them was preposterous in itself. Once more, the sheer audacity of Clifford's plan had law enforcement second guessing themselves. One moment he seemed every bit the timid coward who'd roll over on any of his fellow prisoners for a pat on the head, but the next he would burst out into some wild action that nobody could predict. There would be no pretending that this was temporary madness in the face of danger to his life amidst riots. It had been calculated and planned meticulously to produce precisely the results that Clifford had wanted.

And it was true this time around, Clifford had a plan beyond just running. No more aimless wandering or hoping that trouble would pass him over. He was getting out of Canada and starting over somewhere that he had a clean record. Everyone in the Great White North could hunt for him to their heart's content, because he was going someplace where nobody knew his name.

This time he fled the town with plans for heading south. He went inland first, avoiding population centres as much as possible to avoid any sightings leading the police to him. Practising his craft as a burglar once more, he broke into rural properties, leaving behind valuables but stealing survival essentials: tinned food, clothes, blankets, even a pistol.

He had no intention of going back to prison. If he could achieve his freedom without hurting anyone, then he would do so, but nobody was going to be standing in his way. He was going to be free.

Luckily, the odd pattern of his thefts gave the police a clear lead on the direction that Clifford was headed. By New Westminster, the border posts had been alerted to his status as an escaped prisoner, but further east there was nothing so formal to prevent him passing over. It was not incredibly surprising that he was fleeing over the American border, given how close it was to New Westminster and the prison, but his planning to pass south further out into the wilds was certainly unexpected. Patrols were mobilised to keep watch for him on both sides of the border, but they had an absolutely massive stretch of land to cover, and he was liable to slip between their fingers unless something changed. Once he was over the border into America, it would be increasingly difficult to track him. The population was so huge that Clifford could change his name and vanish into the crowd.

Exhaustion was dogging him by the time that he came into sight of the provincial park where he meant to finally break south. There were paths heading south along the border here; he'd seen them on maps back in the prison. It would be so simple to just dawdle along them until they ran out and take a step into the wilderness beyond. His route was memorised. His goal was set. He had no time for doubt.

When he rounded the first bend in the forest path, he froze. Two teenagers were there, chatting to one another as if they were just out for a walk in the park. Which, admittedly, they were. They had no idea of the trouble that had just found its way to them. Not until Clifford's eyes bugged out of his head and he yanked the pistol from his belt.

He did not aim the gun at them—they would be very clear about that when they later had to file their police reports—but he did wave it about, yelling threats and damning them for ruining everything. He made them swear on their lives that they wouldn't tell anybody that they'd seen him, then took off running. Of course, the first thing that they did was sprint for civilisation and call the police about the maniac in the woods running around menacing people with a gun for no reason whatsoever.

The police took down the description and immediately realised that they finally had a sighting of the elusive Clifford Olson Junior. The local police and border patrol were deployed with all haste, and before Clifford could even come into sight of the borderline that he'd imagined thick and red across the forest floor, they were swarming all through the provincial park and beyond.

Clifford kept his pistol in hand but secreted himself on the forest floor, covering himself in a thick layer of fallen leaves and remaining perfectly still. He had the patience to outwait this, just as he'd had the patience to outlast the police the last time around. He knew he could become invisible, and if one of the roaming officers stepped directly on him by pure chance, that was why he had the gun. He was not going back to jail. Not without a fight.

Even as he lay perfectly still in the leaves, watching the legs of the police pass him by, sometimes mere feet away, he was certain that he would evade them again. Unbeknownst to him, he was already in America. The police roaming about were not the Canadian officers he'd run rings around for so long, but Washington police, forced out of town to come help clean up somebody else's mess. It was the sort of thing that made a police officer annoyed: clashing jurisdictions, no real opportunity to prove themselves, but plenty of opportunity to catch the blame if the prisoner slipped free. In fact, there was probably only one officer in the whole forest who was happy to be there.

Tiger the police dog strolled right up to Clifford where he lay and started barking. He looked up into the dog's face, and with a sigh, he dropped his pistol. He wasn't going to shoot a dog just for being a dog.

In moments he was completely surrounded, with guns pointed at him, and he was carted to Blaine, Washington, to be processed and then returned to the Old BC Penitentiary.

Funnily enough, proving himself so untrustworthy to his jailors made him seem much more palatable to his fellow prisoners once more. Men who would have stabbed him to death a few months before now cornered him to hear the story of his cunning escape, clapping him on the back and applauding his guts. He was accepted back into the good graces of the prison community, and he immediately began abusing that position of trust to try and get others in deeper trouble so that he could shave more time off his sentence. He was the warden's favourite informer after all, and that was why they had gone to bat for him time and time again, keeping him from the worse punishments that the courts could have inflicted. Even after almost making it out of the country during his latest escape, he still wasn't back up to the full ten years he was meant to be serving out to begin with. Both guards and prisoners put their trust in Clifford, and he betrayed them all time and time again.

In the years that were to come, Clifford went back and forth from Old BC Penitentiary with startling regularity. He made one more escape attempt, resulting in an extension to his sentence, then he began to whittle away at that extended sentence in the same way that he always had. Funnily enough, after all of his escape attempts through the years, he was actually freed from Old BC by an administrative problem. The prison was in a poor state of repair due to its age, barely suitable for use by the time that Clifford was incarcerated there for the first time, so by his third or fourth time around, years later, whole wings had to be closed due to the structural damage that had been done by the passing years. Electrical systems failed with regularity, leaving prisoners in the pitch black for hours upon hours, the roof sprung leaks, and there was constant trouble with the plumbing, exacerbated by the deliberate efforts of some prisoners to sabotage the system and cause more strife for the guards.

As a result of this dire state of affairs, it was decided that the prison would be cut back in scale to only utilise a central core of rooms that were in good repair, with the excess prisoners being shunted either to other facilities or temporary placements with work-gangs and the prefab housing provided to them, or they'd be offered early release on parole if they had a proven track record of good behaviour.

Clifford inexplicably qualified in the latter category despite being a known flight risk by every member of staff. He had his day in court, was issued with strict instructions on how he should conduct himself if he meant to remain out of prison for any length of time, and then he was released with nothing to his name but a charitable donation of a suit to cover his nakedness.

His freedom was short-lived. While he kept up his end of the arrangement by dutifully appearing at his parole officer's desk every week, he let it down somewhat by spending every other moment of his week committing crimes or planning them. By the time that the police arrested him, Clifford was wanted on charges varying from assault and armed robbery to breaking and entering and forgery. He was picked up for driving while impaired after drinking a fair portion of his ill-gotten gains and then all of the other charges were brought down on him once the police search pinned him at the centre of a morass of crimes.

Back to Old BC he went, one of the last few prisoners being held there. Back to his old cell, which, as luck would have it, was still one of the ones in operation despite all that had come to pass. While it would have seemed logical for the warden and guards to lose faith in him after his swift return to prison, the fact of the matter was that he was of considerably more use to them inside the walls of the jail than he was to society outside of them. Tipping the scales even further in their favour, Clifford had taken his previous early release as a clear thank you from the prison staff for all his diligent hard work, blaming himself for getting caught again rather than law enforcement for catching him.

He began to feed the guards information on his fellow inmates, but by now the Old BC population was so small that it became immediately apparent which social circles were being testified against, and a simple process of elimination put the blame firmly on Clifford. His life was at risk in the prison once this news came out, but rather than attempting to isolate or transfer Clifford until the hubbub calmed down, once again, Clifford was offered early parole. Little more than a year into his sentence.

Out in the world, Clifford lacked any structure or order to his life; in prison he had a very clear purpose and goal—getting out. Yet that was not to say that some of his skills were not transferrable. While he was in prison, he kept himself out of trouble by reporting on others for the guards, and what were the police force if not guards for the outside world? It was not long before

Clifford Olson was one of the best informants that the British Columbia police had at their disposal, sharing every detail of his low-life friends' plans with the police, except for those crimes he was planning on participating in himself. No matter what had happened, Cliff would be the first one that the police picked up, but no charges ever stuck to him. Clearing crimes was more important to the police than any one charge that they might attach to him, and it wasn't as though he didn't offer up more than enough scapegoats to serve prison time for the crimes that the police were quietly confident he had committed himself.

From then on, his relationship with the police was always transactive rather than combative. So long as he brought them something worthwhile relating to a more interesting case, he could walk away from almost any crime with just a slap on the wrist.

Of course, there were limits to what the police were willing to give. There were diminishing returns on the information that Clifford offered up. Tossing the same people under the bus over and over again became pointless. After a certain point, there was a certainty of guilt with Clifford's scapegoats, and while he did his best to expand his social circle beyond the dregs of society who would accept him, the higher class of criminal were more discerning about who they welcomed into their confidence.

So, it should come as no surprise that the man who was forever taking risks soon spent more goodwill than he was earning. He was still earning his primary income through crime but was slowly shifting away from offences that relied on his hands toward transgressions that relied more on his mouth. Burglaries and muggings gave way to entering under false pretences, fraud, and forgery. Crimes that had the potential to earn him more money with less risk, and without any of the violence that seemed to make judges and juries so upset. He might have been destroying lives, but so long as he didn't break the skin, the world seemed to care considerably less.

Of course, he was constantly breaking the conditions of his parole as a result of his crimes, and while the police were happy to smooth things over for him with his parole officer in exchange for his assistance after they'd picked him up, some of his many misdemeanours slipped through the gaps. Each time that they did, Clifford slipped back into jail.

The Old BC Penitentiary was closed by the time that he was taken back into custody, so his new home away from home became the Prince Albert Penitentiary in Saskatchewan. While the Old BC had been a high security prison throughout, the PA was a different beast. Originally a medium security prison, with the steady inflow of dangerous offenders, in part perpetuated by the closure of the Old BC, parts of it had been haphazardly converted to high security areas. The result was a prison unlike anything that Clifford had ever experienced—some parts identical to how he used to live, but other parts almost entirely unobserved. The lower security translated into a much higher rate of low-scale criminality among the residents. The place was rife with drugs, illicit trading, and gangs in a way that Clifford just was not used to after so long in lockdown conditions.

Still, he saw no reason that he couldn't go on playing things exactly the same as he always had. Making contact with the guards and warden early into his stint, offering to trade them information for special treatment and early parole.

At once, he set about enveloping himself in the culture of the prison, finding himself shunted around from group to group constantly by his refusal to declare any sort of allegiance to the gangs that ruled the place. He got as close as he could to where the illegal activity was happening but found himself stonewalled unless he was willing to prove his loyalty in some way, typically by committing the kind of crime that would get more time heaped on his sentence when he was actively trying to whittle it down.

Still, his diligent prying eventually paid off. He couldn't get into the gangs, but he could watch the prisoners in the places that the guards could not. It took him less than a month to compose a list of all the drug couriers in the prison and pass them along to the warden. He was promised that he would see a substantial reduction in his sentence for his good work, once the searches were made and his finger-pointing was proved to be more than just spite.

Returned to the prison population, Clifford saw it all unfolding for the first time. The guards rushing in and wrestling men to the ground, their cells being torn apart. Clothes being ripped off them to expose the drugs smuggled beneath them. He was as horrified as any of his fellow prisoners at the brutality of it all, but internally he thanked his lucky stars that those same guards were on his side and would be around to protect him if anybody got wind of who was responsible for this crackdown. The addicts of the prison were enraged to find their supply cut off. The gangs, who made so much of their money and won so much of their influence through the drug trade, were beyond furious, silently closing down operations and closing ranks until the leak could be discovered.

There were several things that Clifford had not accounted for in his planning. The first was that with the lower security in this prison, there would be places that the guards did not keep under close observation. The second was that such prevalent smuggling operations and drug trading could not have happened in a prison where at least some of the guards weren't on the gangs' payroll. By the time that the first raids were being made, money was already changing hands, and the name of the informer was being passed along to the leaders of the gangs.

Still convinced that he was protected by anonymity and the guards, Clifford strolled through the prison without a care in the world. He was still smiling and greeting people as he moved around the prison, never realising that they all knew what he'd done. Shortly after the drug trade was closed down, Clifford was cornered by a group of prisoners representing those who felt he had wronged them. They wished to discuss this matter with him. They were quite pointed in their arguments.

Clifford spent several months in the prison hospital following that incident. He had been stabbed seven times. Few of the injuries were life threatening in themselves, but thanks to the amount of human waste that had been smeared on the blades before they were used against him, he suffered multiple infections and fevers. Time passed in a disjointed blur as his body fought off those secondary infections all while he was so heavily dosed with painkillers and antibiotics, he could scarcely remember his own name.

By the time that he was ready to be returned to the prison population, he was up for parole again. His sentence had been greatly reduced in light of his service to the Correctional Service of Canada and reduced again in sympathy after he suffered such terrible injuries as a result of that service. The warden even wrote a letter to the judge in Clifford's favour, stating that it would be a risk to the man's life to be returned to the prison population at this point.

Once more, Clifford was set loose on the world—a wounded animal in part, but a thinking and reasoning human being, too. One who could see that the way he had been leading his life was heading for a dead end at high speed. Someone who needed to change his course but had no idea how that might be done. It was another turning point in his life, when he might have been able to get back on the straight and narrow and pursue something resembling a normal life.

A Place to Call Home

Alcohol and drugs were intimately familiar companions to Clifford when he was out of jail, and if he were to be honest, they were the part of freedom that he missed the most. Pills had always been his preference, as they made him feel less like the junkies and losers he associated with, despite the effects being essentially the same. They were the reason that he ultimately turned to the more blatant crimes that got him into the most trouble. Cunning con jobs and fraud produced infinitely more money in the long term, but they rarely gave him the instant gratification of ready cash exactly when he needed it for his fix.

Clifford didn't want to kick his addictions, exactly, so much as he wanted them to be under his control rather than the other way around. He wanted to indulge when he wanted to indulge and to not need them when he wanted to focus on other things. He wanted his mind, not his base impulses, to rule his body. It was a distinct change of pace, and not one that he was able to strike on the first attempt. Several times, he slipped up and found himself back in police custody. Most of his more white-collar crimes were never convicted, but when he slipped up and burgled a home, he was still the first one that the cops picked up.

He'd serve several more short stints in various prisons, culminating in a return to Prince Albert Penitentiary.

That place held too many bad memories for him. It was the last place where he'd felt powerless, and he could not tolerate that feeling. So, he made a rapid escape only a few weeks after he was incarcerated there. He already knew much of the security, and in particular its blind spots, thanks to long weeks observing drug deals during his last stay. He broke out of the prison as easily as cutting a hole through one of the fences. By the time that the guards realised he was gone and a search was mobilised, Clifford had slipped away into the general population, setting out to master himself and start the new life he had planned without ever looking back.

In the outer municipalities of Richmond-Surrey, he found a place that felt both familiar and fresh. With no friends to fall back on, and no bad habits to fall back into, he rented a place of his own at the New Surrey Village Apartments on the King George Highway. It was August of 1980, and Clifford was now forty years old. His entire adult life had been spent in one prison or another, with scarcely a full year in between prison stints. He had never lived by himself, always preferring to couch surf with his lowlife friends and save his money for more important things, but now that he had a space of his own, he felt like a world of opportunity was opening up before him.

His income was mostly predicated on odd jobs. He was always good with his hands, so he found labouring gigs on construction sites when he could, but when nothing was available, he would do gardening and joinery for cash in hand, even dabbling in plumbing and heating engineering if he thought he could help out. As the weather grew colder and the construction work began to slow, he became ever more reliant on these odd jobs to keep a roof over his head. In pursuit of work, he would post his card on community boards about town. It was when he visited the People's Gospel Church in Surrey to beg permission to post his card that he met Joan Hale.

Joan was a little older than him, but given the rough life he'd lived, she looked considerably younger. Unlike most of the women her age that Clifford encountered doing his busy work, she did not have a wedding ring on her finger, and the two of them seemed to take an instant shine to one another. Or rather, Clifford saw in her the opportunity to get his card put up, so he laid the charm on thick. When she began to awkwardly flirt with him, Clifford realised that, despite his age and spotty history, there were women in the world who might actually be attracted to him, and without even thinking twice about it, he began to flirt back. The two of them set up a dinner date for the same evening, and Clifford got his all-important card posted on the community board, so his mind was put at ease.

Their courtship was not a traditional one, with either side constantly feeling that the other had the upper hand because of their circumstances. Joan had more experience with romance than Clifford, whose own teenage fumbling had been cut tragically short by his incarceration, but she felt like she was at a supreme disadvantage in the dating world because she was recently divorced and painfully vulnerable as a result.

Clifford gave away very little about himself, hinting that he'd been in a little trouble through the years, but never quite revealing himself to her entirely. Meanwhile, he used all of his social wiles to extract every bit of information that he could out of Joan about her own life and history, something that she found intensely flattering. Nobody had ever cared about her that much. She had always felt like an afterthought, a secondary player in the lives of more important people. With Clifford, it was as though the sun shone only for her. Like she was the centre of his universe.

So it was that he learned that she had divorced her last husband because he was an abusive alcoholic, using her like a punching bag, and that she was living off of the court settlement that she received from that divorce in a state of relative comfort. Less comfortable than she'd been accustomed to, but infinitely more comfortable than Clifford had ever experienced in his life.

All of the little stories that he extracted from her built up into a more solid picture of the person she was, and how close to her limits she needed to be pushed before she would break.

With that knowledge in mind, he began to push. At first, he was gently pressuring her into a more physical relationship than she was ready to pursue. Then he was pushing to move in with her. He talked his way around all of her concerns until he had her convinced that half of the time it was she who had initiated sex or started the conversation, thus gaslighting her into believing that she was the one relentlessly pursuing him rather than the other way around. That is not to say that the two of them didn't enjoy the courtship. Clifford treated her with a level of respect she'd never had in her married life, and he seemed to bombard her with signs of his affection whenever she felt her faith in him wavering.

Within a few months of meeting one another, they were cohabiting. Living in sin, as Joan called it. What had started off as a simple con job for Clifford had now taken on a life of its own. At first, it was simply because the settlement that she was receiving from her ex-husband was not delivered in a lump sum that Clifford could easily uplift and depart with, but gradually it became something else. He found that he enjoyed being waited on by his girlfriend. He appreciated her affection and her worship. She did what she was told, when she was told to do it, and having sex readily available to him whenever he wanted it was the kind of luxury that Clifford hadn't experienced since he was raping little boys back in the borstal.

His sexual awakening had been twisted with brutality and violence; his adult experiences of it had been almost exclusively the same. The kind of gentle loving that he experienced with Joan was so divorced from those feelings that he almost didn't recognise them. He certainly didn't recognise the other feelings that their time together was awakening in him—the softer ones that he'd always thought he was born devoid of. He could see the value in her, the value in her kindness and her calm. All of the things that he did not have in himself, he found in her. To his shock, he was nice to her not just for the sake of manipulating her into giving him what he wanted, or for the sake of making himself feel good, but because he wanted her to feel good. It was revelatory for a person who had spent their entire life focused entirely on their own gratification.

Admittedly, Clifford still had all of the benefits of his selfishness while making these realisations about himself and this relationship. He was living with Joan, living off of the money sent through by her ex-husband, and taking on only the occasional odd job for extra cash when he felt like it. For her part, Joan had suffered so badly at the hands of her ex-husband that even this level of disrespect and lack of care seemed remarkable to her. She praised Clifford to the heavens for the scraps of affection that he gave to her and accepted his barked commands as her due in life. She was not to question him, ever, but that was still infinitely better than the way that her last husband had shoved his every indiscretion in her face, just to show her how utterly powerless and worthless she was to him. Meanwhile, each time Clifford was short with her, she could rest assured that he'd come around soon after, bombing her with love and affection and apologising profusely.

His rented apartment sat empty most of the time, with his retreating there only occasionally when he felt like Joan needed some distance to realise how everything was in fact her fault. It was increasingly feeling like an unnecessary expense, yet still, he kept up his payments on it to make sure that Joan still felt a sense of instability in their relationship. He didn't want her to take his presence for granted, lest he lose some of the worship that he received from her.

Comfortable and safe for the first time in his adult life, Clifford decided that the time had come to relax and enjoy himself a little. He had been ever so careful since his last escape from prison, so intent on building his life to this point that he'd almost entirely abandoned all of his old passions and crimes. Now he finally felt safe enough to explore the world again from this new vantage point.

It was at this point that his apartment would have come in handy, a den for him to retreat to when he'd been out drinking and experimenting with all the fascinating new pills that were available on the black market in the 80s. Unfortunately, he failed to show up to pay his rent. His landlord contacted Joan, thinking that he'd simply forgotten about it, but she was surprised to learn that he wasn't in his abandoned apartment at that exact moment since he hadn't come home to her.

The unfortunate truth of the matter was that Clifford was in jail. A local woman had accused him of rape.

To his good fortune, the police did not consider her to be a very reliable witness, and the case would soon be thrown out, but for a few weeks, he remained in jail awaiting charges.

His victim was a local prostitute. While he had been enjoying the new pleasures of gentler love with his new girlfriend, that did not mean that any of his darker impulses had disappeared overnight. Sex and violence were still intertwined in his psyche, and he needed to act on his impulses lest they continue to build up and build up into something beyond his control.

He had seemed utterly charming when he'd approached the woman in a bar and shown no hesitation in flashing his cash at her when she let it slip that she was a professional. It seemed to her like the evening was going to be mutually beneficial until they were out of their clothes and he looped his belt around her neck. With her so restrained, he had sex with her, pummelling her in the back and kidneys, slapping her around and tossing her about the hourly rented motel room like she was a rag-doll. All of his physical labour through the years had left him with enviable strength, and he had no hesitation in unleashing it all on the poor woman. When he had finally exhausted the seemingly endless well of energy that his new pills had granted him, he finished off inside her and left her a bruised and bloody heap on the motel floor, something that he would later suggest to the police was entirely consensual.

Perhaps he could have walked away from it unscathed if he had just paid her for his time, but he did not, and so as soon as she was able to pull herself together and wrap her torn clothes about her, she limped down to the station to put in a complaint about him, and he was picked up in another bar soon afterwards.

Clifford emerged from the prison fully intent on murdering the woman who had made the allegation against him, but despite a solid day of searching there was no trace of her to be found. He lacked the underworld contacts in his new stomping grounds, so he was unable to pursue her further, but the deep and abiding rage that he felt towards her did not go away. He returned to Joan's waiting arms and she forgave him absolutely everything, not even knowing what he had done nor how lucky the two of them were that the local police had been so lax in their investigation that they hadn't even realised there was still a warrant out for Clifford's arrest after his latest prison breakout.

After their unexpected separation, Clifford realised just how worried he had been about the prospect of losing Joan in the midst of everything else. She was the anchor holding his new life in place and the foundation on which all of his hopes for the future were built. He needed to do something to bind her to him in a more permanent way. The thought that she might just up and leave him over something as stupid as a rumour of him raping a prostitute scared him.

While he was still trying to work out a way to tie them together permanently that didn't overplay his hand, the universe provided him with exactly the solution that he needed. What Joan had mistaken for early menopause turned out to be a pregnancy. They were going to have a child together.

In the elation of this news, all of the mystery of Clifford's disappearance was forgotten, and all of their attention was dragged away from the past toward the future. They started looking for new homes that might accommodate an extra body. They started talking about marriage, something that neither one of them had been too enthusiastic about considering when they were first starting out.

It was decided that the two of them would have to tie the knot before the baby was born to make sure that it didn't suffer the indignity of being born out of wedlock, and a date was set for May of 1981.

With time to spare before the big day, Clifford decided to hit the road and see a bit of the world before settling down. For the first few weeks, he drove through some of his old haunts, recognizing nobody and nothing there, even skirting along the border where he'd once made his haphazard escape over the border, reminiscing about his past and finally ending up in British Columbia.

The Old BC Penitentiary had been decommissioned entirely by this point, and by happenstance, it was open to the public to visit as a kind of morbid tourist attraction. Unable to resist the siren call of his old home, Clifford bought himself a ticket and went for the tour. Now finally things started to feel familiar once more. The water-stained walls, the trampled grounds, and the cold stone beneath his hand all felt like they had when he was a prisoner there. He even made his way through the crowds to peer through the open door of his old cell.

It was there that he was recognised. One of the old guards from the prison had found a new job as a tour guide in the Old BC. Clifford had probably walked past him a half-dozen times throughout the tour with neither man making a connection. With the added context of the cell that Clifford was standing beside, however, the ex-guard immediately made the connection. While he might no longer have been in the service, that did not mean that his friends were not. Or that he didn't still hear news about his old inmates. Particularly old inmates who had escaped from jail and were still at large.

A phone call was made, and by the time that Clifford walked out of the doors of the Old BC a free man, the police were waiting for him all over again. He had a month slapped onto what was left of his original sentence, and he was confined in the Matsqui Institution in Abbotsford.

As far as his fiancé knew, he was still doing his grand bachelor party road trip, and he had no intention of disabusing her of that illusion any time soon. He still had a few months to count down before the wedding. All that he had to do to be out and home in time was to say his vows. There was no attempt to inveigle himself into the criminal gangs, to seek out friends that he could turn in for time off his sentence, or anything else. He kept his head down, he did his time, and he got out on parole exactly when he expected to with his record as a model prisoner.

A quick cross-country jaunt later and he was back in Joan's arms, although he was held at a distance by the bump of her rapidly growing stomach. Despite the lack of contact, Joan had inexplicably never lost faith that he'd return in time to wed her. She believed in Clifford in a way that nobody ever had and nobody ever would again. It was almost enough to make him believe in himself, in the dreams for the future that he'd idly dreamed while staring up at the ceiling of his prison cell, waiting for the days to pass.

At the People's Gospel Church in Surrey, the very place where they had first met, the two of them were married on May 15, 1981. His family was notable in their absence. Many of her family had disappeared from her life in the aftermath of her divorce, but the congregation of the church filled every pew in the building and welcomed Clifford into the fold. Just as Joan had accepted him into her life without question, so too did they welcome him into their community. It was almost enough to make him want to live up to the implied promise that he'd be good in return. Almost.

After they were wed, it did not take long for Clifford to rush through the sale of his newly acquired house and relocate them. Rumours still circulated about him after his run-in with the prostitute, and he did not want for his wife or child to overhear either of them.

He found a new job and home, all in one, in the city of Coquitlam, where he was employed by the town as the super for an apartment block on Whiting Way. The apartments were small though suited to the newlywed Olsons just fine for the first few months, but it would not be long before they were house hunting again. The Whiting Way Apartments were adults only. So, with the scheduled arrival of their baby just around the corner, they had to devote an undue amount of time to the search. As it turned out, the baby wasn't the only thing just around the corner. An apartment became available in the complex on Foster Avenue, literally around the corner from the Whiting Way apartments that Clifford managed, and they relocated all of their meagre belongings in just a few quick jaunts back and forth in the car.

The couple were settled not a moment too soon because their newborn baby Stephen Olson arrived just a few days later.

Just as Clifford had found a new capacity for love in his relationship with Joan, so did he learn new things about himself at the sight of the wriggling pink baby in his arms. All of the things that he thought he had missed out on in life, all of the things that regular folks aspired to, were now his. He had a normal life. A wife, a child, a job, an apartment. There was no outstanding warrant for his arrest or any doom dogging his footsteps. He had a chance now to live a good life. To do good things and leave a positive mark on the world.

He went to church with Joan every Sunday, and there could scarcely have been a better scholar of the Bible than him. He could quote passages from memory better than the pastor—though of course, he didn't mention that this was because it had been his only reading material for the many months he had in solitary confinement.

More than just doing the due diligence of going to church, Clifford seemed to take the spirit of Christian charity to heart. There were many underprivileged children living in the same apartment building as him and his family, and while he spoiled his child rotten with gifts, he would just as often come back home with a big sack of toys that he'd hand out to the other children on the block. He couldn't make such grand gestures every day, but he always had a piece of candy to give to the kids who saw no kindness from their own parents. It was hard to picture a more beloved man than Clifford Olson in those days.

At one point a little girl from the neighbourhood went missing, and he got into his car and drove around into the early hours of the morning looking for her. He seemed to be constantly chatting with the little girls in the neighbourhood, complimenting them and offering them little treats, and while a few of the parents found that suspicious, when it was viewed in combination with all of his other charitable works, it was difficult to find much basis for fear.

They were wrong to have doubted their instincts.

The Other Side

Clifford had been living a double life. Ever since his night with the prostitute had almost ended in everything falling apart, his sex drive—and his violent urges—had continued to grow. The murderous rage that he'd felt after being exposed and publicly accused of doing more or less exactly what he'd done had not abated either. If he had crossed paths with the prostitute who had so shamed him, it was likely that he would have murdered her in broad daylight and damn the consequences. While she would never appear in his life or his story again, that seed of vengeful wrath became a dominant force in his psyche, merging with his other violent and sexual impulses until it was almost impossible for him to function sexually without at least the implication of violence. To begin with, he had expressed this by treating his wife ever more roughly, but with the advancement of her pregnancy that was no longer an option. He had to get these impulses out. Somehow, he had to expel the demons that clouded his thoughts so that life could go on and he could give Joan and Stephen the lives they deserved.

Immediately after he had been released from jail following his brutalization of the prostitute, and after he had heard from Joan that they were going to have a child together, he went out to celebrate. He drank just as he had before, he took pills just as he had before, he worked himself up into a veritable frenzy just as he had before.

Christine Weller was twelve years old on that fateful evening in November. Earlier in the day, she had escaped the general malaise that hung over the motor court in Surrey, BC, where her unemployed parents lived, to go window shopping at the local mall. She couldn't afford to buy anything—she could never afford to buy anything—but even wandering around beneath the hum of the strip lights looking at all the things she would never be able to have was better than staying at home and looking at all the things she didn't want.

She lingered at the mall for as long as she could, long after all the friends that she'd met up with wanted to go home, until finally the last of them was departing and, concerned that she wouldn't make it home in time for the non-existent dinner that her parents would have on the table, gave her a loan of his bicycle. Despite not having one of her own, the devoted tomboy was more than comfortable in the saddle, thanking her friend and pedalling furiously away towards home. It was the last time that she would be seen alive.

Somewhere along her route, she was intercepted by Clifford. While it seems likely that he would have initially attempted to win her over with kind words, the way that he had so many others, Christine was a little more canny than most of his victims. She was from a rougher part of town, where the interest of an older man was treated as suspicious rather than flattering. At some point she turned down his offer to drive her home, likely citing the bicycle that he had no room for in his car as an excuse. At this point, Clifford switched to a new tack.

Drawing a knife, he pressed it against the girl's throat and forced her into the car. He then kicked the bicycle off the road, into the bushes, and returned to the vehicle, putting the knife back to her neck on the opposite side when she attempted to escape. Both of these threats left superficial cuts on her neck, not deep enough to put her life in danger, but deep enough to hurt, and to bleed, so that she knew Clifford meant business.

He took her to the Fraser River Dikes in Richmond, an area he knew would be scarcely populated at this time of year given the chilly weather, and he dragged her out of the car by the hair before flinging her down onto the grass and mud. While it is likely, given what is known of Clifford, that he attempted to rape her, there was no forensic evidence found after the fact to prove that he was successful. But even if he did not penetrate the sanctity of her body in that way, he found many other means of ingress. With the same knife he'd used to threaten and coerce her, he began to stab her. He held her down by her neck as she tried to squirm away, feeling her hot blood running over his palms, but his attention was on her body. Over and over he thrust the knife down into her, a fresh blossom of blood appearing on her clothes each time. The blood pulsing against his hand slowed and stopped, but still, he kept on going. Ten times, he hammered his knife home. Twice cutting into her heart, four times into her liver. Over and over, long beyond the point of killing her. Long beyond the point of anything resembling sanity. He stabbed and he stabbed that innocent little girl for no better reason than it made him feel good about himself.

When Christine didn't return home that night, her parents did not notice, but several days later they reported her absence to the police, who took one look at her family life and filed her as a runaway.

It would not be until Christmas morning that the truth would come out, when a dog-walker heading along the Fraser River was dragged off the path by his dog and they came upon the gruesome scene of a decomposing and desecrated corpse.

The police finally lurched into action with this discovery. They brought up a list of all known convicted sex offenders in the area and took photos of these potential killers to all the places Christine had last been seen in an effort to uncover any potential witnesses. Clifford slipped through the investigation's fingers, in no small part because the police did not look on him as a criminal—they looked on him as a resource. All of his time spent helping them out through the years had paid off. He had an easy manner about him when faced with interrogation, and it appeared to the investigators that if he'd had any information about the crime, he'd have been delighted to part with it and earn some goodwill or reward money.

The rush of the kill was enough to keep Clifford sated for a time. He had always felt like he was the smartest guy in any room, and now his already overwhelming confidence was bolstered with the knowledge that he could literally get away with murder. The net result was that every other part of his life began to drastically improve. Even his relationship with his wife was greatly soothed as he no longer felt any compulsion to assert his will on her.

That universal improvement to his daily life was another kind of high that he was happy to ride along on without overthinking or having any real desire to deviate from. Without the lows, he no longer needed to chase the highs. He refrained from drinking too much, from popping pills or from seeking out pleasure in the arms of women of dubious virtue for several months following the murder of Christine. He had the memory of her body opening beneath his knife to keep him warm at night.

Yet, with the spring of '81, there came a renewal not only in the natural world but in Clifford's awful hungers. His relationship with his fiancé became increasingly strained as her pregnancy went on and the regular 'relations' that they'd both enjoyed up until then began to dry up. At the same time, a whole new pool of potential victims had opened up when they moved into their apartment in South Surrey. He courted them out in the open with gifts and sweets and treats, gaining a reputation as a kindly man, and showing no hint of any untoward advances towards the children playing in the streets. He was more than a little bit beloved. All because nobody who received the full weight of his attentions ever lived to tell the tale.

It was an awful weight of temptation on a man who had never been very good at resisting his own darker desires.

With his reputation for kindness, when he offered thirteen-year-old Coleen Daignault a job at his work site, she didn't even hesitate to take him up on it. The possibility of cash in her pocket was a better prospect than anybody else in the neighbourhood had, and she was bored out of her mind sitting around on the street with nobody to play with while the rest of her buddies went off to school.

She was caught up in his boisterous excitement, so when he cracked open his glove box and offered her a swig of schnapps to celebrate the new opportunity, she was happy to drink it, feeling extremely grown up, having a drink with her new boss and heading off to her new job. She didn't know exactly where they were going, and after another swig from the bottle, she didn't much care. She didn't really care about anything anymore. Everything just seemed like too much work. Even sitting up in the car and carrying on the inane conversation was too much for her. Sleep sounded better. Just a quick nap so she was ready to get to work when they arrived. Just a little rest, with her head vibrating against the window of his truck. Nobody would mind that.

A blissful darkness took her over. There was none of the dull stomach-churning that she'd been feeling since she took that drink. None of the aches and pains as her body strained against the rest it so desperately needed. All of the pain in her life just faded away.

Then abruptly it came back.

The pain was sharp, insistent. It dragged her out of her stupor and set her flailing. Her eyes snapped open, but even though she was in blinding agony, she could already feel them starting to slip back shut again. The sun was shining down on her face from on high. Sharp stones and dirt were digging into her back, scrapes and scuffs, a jerked shoulder where she'd been dragged out of the cab of the truck. Between her legs she could feel something burning, a pain almost worse than the sharp one in her head.

There was cold air nipping at her legs, touching her in the wet hurt burning place between them. It should have cooled that pain, but it just made it flare. What had happened to her? Had she been in a car accident? Was she dying all alone out here? Fear crept up and stole her voice, even as the dark tried to drink her down again. She couldn't move. She strained with all her might, but no part of her body seemed to be under her command. It was bad. The accident must have been really bad to leave her like this. Paralyzed. Only her eyes seemed to be under her control, so she swung her lurching vision about, searching desperately for anyone who might help.

And there he was, her saviour. Mr Olson. He looked rough, too. Dishevelled, sweating, and his usually slick hair was all awry. He was staring down at her. She could see him panting. She hoped that he was okay. She hoped that he could get help. She hoped in vain.

Clifford hefted the hammer in his hand and brought it down on the raped little girl's head once again. The roofie he'd slipped her in the drink should have been enough to keep her still until all of this was over, but now he was finding a new perverse delight in seeing her move. Each time the hammer struck her skull, it was like a message shot out through all the nerves in her body, setting limbs flopping and piss flowing.

He laughed out loud at the sight of it. No need to stay quiet out here. That was why he'd picked the abandoned lot to do his dirty deeds.

It was all good fun to Clifford now. He'd gotten what he needed, or at least he'd gotten most of it. Now all he had to do was finish her off and clean up, but there was no hurry. Nobody was expecting him anywhere and he had all the time in the world to just... experiment. His next hit was softer, angled to the side of her skull, and he burst out laughing as the leg and arm on the other side flopped in response. He was a scientist now, experimenting on this soon-to-be corpse to see what the body would do. He was the silver hammer man, like the Beatles sang about. He hummed that tune to himself as he swung again, and again, and again. Harder and harder and harder.

The girl couldn't scream, but each blow drove what air she had in her lungs out. A huff and a mealy groan. Over and over he drove the air from her. This was better than the sex. Better than the drugs. Better than the drink. This was everything. Total power. Total control over her. Whatever he wanted he could take. With the last two blows he went all out. He let himself finally do what he'd been building up to all along.

All the strength that he hid every day, all the power and the violence that he had contained inside of him—he let it all out. Her pretty little head broke, the skull crumpling into the brain, once, and then again on the other side. Two hammer blows to end it all.

He could see the brain inside her ruined skull now. The hammer had punched in clean. Just a quick swipe moved the blood and hair aside and let him see inside to that most secret part of her. The part that no man would have ever seen if he hadn't taken the initiative. He was more than a scientist; he was an explorer. Going places that cowards didn't dare to go. He should have been famous for what he was doing, not hiding it from the world. He was a god amongst men.

The god amongst men wrapped his victim up and tossed her into the bed of his truck before driving out of town to dump her in the wilderness. He'd learned from the mistakes of his first kill. He wasn't leaving the body anywhere it might be found to bring police interest down on him, and he had worked out his script perfectly. The job offer, the roofied liquor, the smile, the business cards, all of it worked together to fill his victims up with the same confidence that flooded him all day, every day. He could kill whenever he wanted. He could get away with anything.

To the police, the two missing girls—one now known to be murdered—did not immediately set off any alarms. It was, of course, tragic that one girl was dead, but it did not follow that anything had happened to Coleen Daignault. She was another latchkey kid, left to her own devices while both parents worked. It seemed much more likely to the police that she was a runaway than that the mysterious killing of some girl a town over happened to be related.

They did their due diligence, of course, interviewing folks that knew her and even chatting with the super for her building about her comings and goings. Clifford was happy to tell them everything that he knew about the girl's usual routine and family life, and the fact that he was a career criminal didn't come into the conversation once.

Even as the police investigation was stumbling into action, Clifford killed again. He was powerful, he was joyous. Why should he flinch away from doing what he loved? He picked up the sixteen-year-old Daryn Johnsrude in his old stomping grounds of Westminister, immediately running through the very same routine that had hooked Coleen less than a week before. A job offer, a celebratory drink. It all came so easily to him now. Like he was running the script of one of his old cons. A man like him, folks looked at him and assumed he was always chasing money. They'd hold their wallets closer and button shut their purses, but nobody suspected that what he was after was worth so much more than gold.

The boy had only arrived in town a couple of days before. He'd been aimlessly wandering the mall without any friends or company. Clifford barely even had to bait the hook to get him to climb into the car with him. He had a pack of beer settled on the bench between them. The boy never saw the pill being dropped in his.

Clifford drove the unconscious child to Deroche, where he already had a kill-site picked out. Once again, he raped his victim while they were completely lost to the drugs, but this time around, he made an extra effort to cause pain, to stir the flopping boy from his sleep. He wanted to see the fear in the boy's eyes.

Sexual preferences were not relevant to Clifford. He was not gay any more than he was straight—he was a predator, and any human being would do to sate his gradually combining lusts for flesh and blood.

Daryn was more resilient than the little girls that he had butchered before. He became aware of what was happening to him sooner; he survived the brutal assault for longer. Of course, no small part of that was by design. Clifford worked his way up the boy's naked body with the hammer instead of leaping to the big finish, breaking bones and bruising flesh all the way up before finally dealing killing blows to the boy's head.

Foot on the Accelerator

While the connection between his previous victims had not been recognised by the investigators, there were individuals who were familiar with serial murder that had begun to collate information to devise a pattern to the killings, in case it should turn out that they were related after all. The murder of Daryn Johnsrude ruined all of that. Serial killers are almost always very particular about their victims, rarely crossing gender or race lines once a pattern of murder has been established. By switching so soon, Clifford destroyed any pattern that might have been forming.

His switch from a knife to a hammer as a murder weapon would also serve to layer on confusion when bodies were finally discovered. He broke the known mould of a serial killer, and that made him infinitely more difficult to catch. The same chaotic energy that drove him to behave the way that he did, and that ruined any opportunity he might have had at progress in a normal life, also masked him from detection.

With the wedding coming up, his murderous activities wound down. He had too many things to attend to in his day-to-day life to go tearing off on another bender. Daryn's body was found entirely by coincidence by some hikers during that down period, but with Colleen's remaining undiscovered, there was once again no pattern for the police to detect. Of the two bodies that had been found, there was no obvious connection. One had been stabbed, one was the victim of a brutal beating and homosexual rape. There was even an age disparity between the dead children that should have put them in separate victim groups, one for paedophiles and one for ephebophiles who target older children in the midst of puberty. Everything pointed to the victims being unrelated except by geography. This time they didn't even bother to interview Clifford. He had no record for bothering boys.

So, Clifford stood in church in his finely pressed suit, holding hands with the mother of his child and bathing in the collective adoration of the community as he recited Bible passages by rote while Colleen still lay rotting in the middle of nowhere.

After just four days of matrimonial bliss, Clifford was ready to kick off the real celebration. He slipped into the usual routine of cruising around in his car with a drink in hand and pills already dissolved into his system before he turned the ignition.

Like the stars had aligned for him, he saw a girl with her thumb stuck out for a ride as he trawled through suburban Langley. He'd barely even started working himself up yet, and the perfect opportunity had presented itself.

Sandra Wolfsteiner was sixteen years old. She had been at her boyfriend's house, and the two of them had been arguing, leaving her without a ride home. Her curfew was fast approaching, and while she was lurking around a bus stop that would take her in the right direction, she had no idea of the schedule for public transport out in suburbia, and she was more than a little anxious that she wouldn't make it in time. She didn't want to fight with her boyfriend and her parents at the same time. She needed somebody to be in her corner.

Then, like a miracle, along came Clifford in his truck, smiling away. A miracle in her time of need. He didn't have to come up with any of his usual spiel; he didn't have to convince her of a thing. All he had to do was welcome the girl in and nod when she asked if he was heading her way.

There was no need for cleverness or tricks when he offered her a drink. She was having a bad day and took the flask from him without a second thought, knocking back enough chloral hydrate in one swig to knock out a grown man. When it made her feel queasy, she made a joke of it. When she felt drowsiness creeping up on her, she curled up in a little ball on the seat.

She'd looked at him like he was a miracle, coming along to save her from her troubles, but now it seemed the tables were flipped. She was everything that he wanted and needed in that moment, and he didn't even have to try to get it.

Out by the Chilliwack Lake, with the sun long down and her curfew long past, she didn't even stir as he climbed on top of her in the long grass. He was far from done after the rape. In his fallow time between killings, ideas had been bubbling in Clifford's head. Things that he wanted to try. Experiments.

With his hammer in one hand and a five-inch iron spike in the other, he set to work on her skull, driving it into her brain in different places to see just how much control he could gain over her spasmodically twitching body. Perhaps she would have recovered from the massive dose of drugs if he had not, but he would have killed her in some other way if it were not for the spike.

Under the seat of his truck, he had begun constructing a little selection of tools for his fun time. A syringe that he was going to use to inject air bubbles to cause embolisms. The spike that he'd use to perform brutal brain surgeries. The tranquilisers he'd use to knock his victims out. A length of rope he planned to use as a garotte. There was a whole world of excitement just waiting for him. So many little games to play. So many new things to learn.

At some point throughout Clifford's experiments with the spike, Sandra died. He went on playing with her corpse for some time, amazed that he could still draw reactions from the rapidly cooling body with a twist of the spike, listening to her death rattle and then compressing different parts of her to see what other sounds could still be drawn out. In death as in life, she was an object to be toyed with. He buried her in a shallow grave, having learned from his mistakes with the previous victims. Simply dumping them in isolated areas had proven not to help to conceal them from his old nemesis: dogs.

With the birth of his son, Clifford once again slowed down. He was so enamoured with the baby and with his new life that he put a halt to his drinking, drugs, and murders. His emotional state stabilised, he had no need to go out seeking a high when he was so contented in his life. There could be no question that he still had the desire to do evil, that he longed for it and lusted after it with all of his being, but with the tiny, wrinkled baby nestled in his arms, he could not tear himself away for long enough to act.

He didn't act with all of his dark desires building up inside of him, bleeding through to the other side of his double life. After so long carefully partitioning his life into the predatory side and the public one, he slipped up.

One of the children that he doted on in the apartment complex was a four-year-old girl. In the midst of his baby frenzy and the mounting pressures of repressing his urges, he fell into a new routine with her, one that he seemed suspiciously confident in performing given that he would later claim to have never approached a child so small. Plying her with gifts. Isolating her from her peers. He began to pressure her to spend time alone with him in places where nobody else could see. He had things he wanted to show her. Things he wanted to teach her.

She may have been a tiny child, but she was savvy enough to recognise that something was not right. Her parents, by comparison, found it all too easy to work out what their super was up to. The police were called, and questions had to be answered, but once again, Clifford's familiarity with police interrogation and calm demeanour completely disarmed the investigators. He managed to play the whole thing off as a misunderstanding, a little girl repeating fragments of a conversation out of order and causing all manner of fuss over nothing at all.

Clifford was so charming that not only were the police convinced, the parents of the little girl bought it, too. She was punished for spreading lies, he promised to keep his distance from her to prevent any confusion in the future, and they all parted looking more sheepish than furious that a little girl had almost been violated by a violent sexual predator.

Still, that close brush with the law was sufficient to make Clifford realise that the part of him that longed for blood could not be stuffed under the bed and forgotten about so easily. It was not a desire to dominate others, to kill and master their bodies—it was a need, pulsing and desperate within his head.

Not to mention that the usual burning desire for revenge on the world for trying to tell him off flared up all over again, just as it had with the prostitute. It was a strange quirk of his personality that when he did wrong and suffered the consequences of his actions he took it quite amicably, but when he slipped through the fingers of the law, he became indignant and wanted to lash out, as though he not only expected punishment for his crimes but wanted it somehow. Deserved it.

Though he was entirely self-serving and self-obsessed, this odd flare up could almost be considered his conscience at work. That, or he was so accustomed to time in jail by this point in his life that he subconsciously sought it.

So, with an anger and a lust in him that his loving family life could not touch, Clifford took to the roads once more, more than a month since the last time that the universe had seen fit to drop a victim in his lap.

While he usually drank, took his pills, and drove out to a neighbouring town to do his hunting, on June 21st, he was scarcely out of his own neighbourhood in Coquitlam before he saw his new prey.

Ada Court was walking home along the North Road after finishing up her babysitting job. She was tired, but happy to have some money in her pocket. There was a spring in her step when the stranger's truck pulled up alongside her and he called over, offering her a lift.

Looking at him, there didn't seem to be anything dangerous about him. He looked intensely amicable, with a little chubbiness that reminded the girl of an uncle. She almost asked him if they were related before wondering if it was rude. He rolled alongside her while she walked, and they had as nice a conversation as she'd ever managed with an adult. Him asking what she'd been up to, her politely answering, never committing to taking a ride with him, but not turning him down either. She was pretty tired, and the walk was long. Eventually he switched tactics, talking to her about the job she'd just done, asking if she wanted to make some more money. He reckoned he had some administrative work that might suit a girl like her.

She was 13. Babysitting was all she'd ever done, and she said as much, but he wasn't to be put off so easily. Smart girl like her, he was sure she could handle it. If she had five minutes to spare, he could interview her now, see if she had the skills he needed. He could even give her a ride home while they talked. Two birds, one stone.

As it turned out, just a few minutes into the ride he was more than satisfied that she'd be able to handle the work that he had on offer, and she was almost overwhelmed at the prospect of all the pocket money she'd be making for just an hour or two one evening each week. She'd be able to quit the babysitting jobs, maybe start going to the pictures with her friends again. This chance meeting was going to completely change her life.

The guy seemed as delighted as she was that he'd finally found somebody to fill the role. Feeling very proud of herself, very mature, and unwilling to annoy her new boss, Ada took a swig from the drink that was offered to her and immediately felt sick. She did her best to keep it down, even as her body struggled to reject it, and the jolly man in his bright suit laughed at her discomfort. The world shifted sideways, the shadows of the evening stretching and coiling until they'd enveloped her entirely and there was nothing left but darkness. She was a tiny girl, and the dose was almost lethally strong. Almost. Clifford didn't want his victims dead until he'd had his fun.

Whatever depravities he exposed her to, it ended the same way. Multiple hammer blows to the skull, smashing through the bone and into the brain. It was possible that she was already dead by then from air embolism, strangulation, beating, or stabbing, but the true nature of this crime would never be entirely exposed because of how well the body was hidden. He had driven the unconscious girl out to Weaver Lake, where he knew that at that time of night there would be nobody for miles, and he had his way with her. Then when his fun was over, he dug a shallow grave and dropped the naked and ruined corpse of the little girl in like he was tossing out the trash.

Heading back home with that done, Clifford did not feel the same satisfaction that he once had. Every kill that he made seemed a little duller than the last. A little less exciting and enticing. Just as he'd developed a resistance to liquor after drinking for too long, and he now had to pop twice as many pills to keep his high going, so too was murder proving to have diminishing returns. There were still parts that he loved: the victims' helplessness, their suffering. But so much of the rest of the process was losing its shine. It was becoming too much like work for him, and nobody hated work quite like Clifford.

He needed more than it was giving him to make it worthwhile. He had to get through every day with his wife and his kid without slipping up and letting any of his other half come through. He had to do his job to keep a roof over their heads. He had to keep up the web of lies so that nobody would notice what he was doing in his off hours. They should have been praising him, worshipping at his feet for the amazing discoveries that he was making, but instead, he had to skulk in the shadows like he was some common criminal.

It wasn't right and it wasn't fair. The longer he went unpunished, the more furious he became with the imbalance of the world. Why wasn't he getting what he deserved?

Added to this already roiling mix of emotions was another failed accusation against him. Another moment of failure on his part, where he preyed on a girl and she managed to survive. A sixteen-year-old was sexually assaulted, with Clifford slipping from his usual fatherly approach to groping molestation without a moment for the girl to change gears. She screamed, she flailed. He was accustomed to victims that were numbed by drugs, not living, breathing, fighting teenagers that stood almost as tall as him.

Not only had she broken free, but she had gone straight to the police. Clifford was hauled out of his bed that night and tossed into a cell that he sat in until the dawn came, waiting for judgement. In the dark of his cell, he laid his plans. They must have known by now that he had killed all those other kids, but he was willing to bet that he could cut a deal if he confessed to everything. That little girl he'd touched up in the apartments was nothing compared to all of that, barely an afterthought. He didn't even think to compose a defence for what he'd done to her until he was being interrogated and he realised, agonisingly slowly, that the police had nothing.

They had the girl, of course, and her account of what had happened and his bleary-eyed confusion about the whole thing. They had the other little girl, the four-year-old who'd made the same accusation and been dismissed out of hand. It wasn't evidence. The girls' statements together looked a little damning, but he'd talked his way out of this once, and he could do it again now that he knew what he was dealing with.

His best lesson in dealing with the police had always been to offer them something so that they could chase that instead of him. Whether it was friends, acquaintances, or downright lies, he'd always tossed out bait, and the hounds had gone chasing. So this time, he gave them his guilt. He'd been messing around with the girl. They'd both been drinking. He hadn't realised that she was so young. All the usual lies that men in that situation told. All the lies that the police had heard a dozen times before. Lies that worked.

He walked out of the police station with a court date and a warning, but like most of these cases, it was liable to evaporate long before it was ever brought before a judge. The victim would have had to relive the experience again and again. She would have had to stand in front of her friends and her family and talk about the disgusting things that Clifford had done to her. Few sixteen-year-olds would have had the courage for that. Fewer still could have looked into the eyes of the man who'd done it and make their accusations.

Still, Clifford walked out a free man with a whole new font of fury overflowing within him. He had already been on the precipice, a junkie with his usual fix held just out of reach, but now this fresh indignity had come along. That was all that it took to push him over the edge.

Season of the Harvest

In July 1981, Clifford killed like he never had before, trying to replace the lack of quality he was finding in tormenting his victims with quantity. He might not be able to reach the same heights as he had when he first killed, but he could maintain a constant flow of adrenaline and excitement instead. Just days after his release from jail, he unleashed hell.

Simon Partington was only nine years old. He was riding his bicycle just a couple of streets away from his house in Surrey, close enough that if he had called out, his mother might very well have heard him. Of course, he did not call out. He was enthralled. With a victim so young, Clifford did not have to resort to promises of jobs or a better future. He didn't even need to do much at all, just offer a little bit of attention and the pretence that he considered the little boy to be mature enough to stop and have a conversation with. He was big and bright and flashy—it didn't take much more to ensnare a child so young.

After some chatter, Simon clambered up into the cab beside Clifford and they shared a beer. After a while longer, Clifford took them for a little drive. There was nothing in the little boy's drink. No poisons or drugs. He was tiny, and Clifford was a full-grown man accustomed to violence. He had no fear that this one would escape him. With just his bare hands he could break little Simon into a hundred pieces.

They drank another beer as they travelled, Simon tipsy and giggling, willing to go along with whatever the older man said, so long as he said it in his comical booming voice. They drove all the way out of town, all the way to the river in Richmond. Then out in the middle of nowhere, with night beginning to fall, Clifford threw the boy down to the ground, and Simon started to cry.

The fall hurt, and he felt funny and sleepy and sick. His new friend was bullying him, and he didn't know why. They'd been having so much fun just a minute before, laughing and talking. Even drinking beer had been fun. It was fizzy like soda, but it tasted funny. And now for no reason at all, he'd shoved him. Picked him up and thrown him.

With one heavy hand spread across the boy's chest, Clifford could feel Simon's heart fluttering like a bird in a cage. He pressed down, and the bones began to bow, bending instead of breaking. Creaking beneath his strength. The boy's sobs slowed as the air was rung from his lungs. Only when the child was silent and still did Clifford ease the crushing pressure. Simon was not unconscious, despite the shallow breaths he was only now managing to take. He had simply stilled so that the pain might end.

It wouldn't.

With the quiet he desired for his work, Clifford began stripping the little boy. When Simon's sobs came, they were muffled. He was afraid and confused and a little bit drunk, but he knew that nothing good could come of the man stripping his clothes away. He struggled only fitfully as Clifford bore down on him again, turning him over as he tore his clothes away, touching him in the places that he was not meant to be touched. Then the pain came. The burning as something was pushed inside him. He cried out then, but the sound was cut short as Clifford's huge hands moved up to encircle the boy's throat.

Simon didn't even have a chance to scream as he was raped and murdered. Clifford had been right enough about the difference in their strength. He crushed the life out of the boy, choking him even as he pushed his way inside. It was all over swiftly compared to the usual slow and arduous torture that Clifford liked to bestow on his victims, but it did not seem brief to Simon. It lasted the rest of his life.

He faded in and out, rising on a crest of agony and falling back into the dark obscurity that he soon came to crave. Each thrust and grunt was punctuated by a tightening of Clifford's grip, pain like nothing that the little boy had ever felt, then the blissful release as the fingers digging into his neck pinched off the supply of blood to his brain. In and out. Light and dark. Until finally, blessedly, he was too far gone into the dark to come back.

The boy was buried in the wet soil by the riverside, sunk into the black, sucking mud, and then Clifford went home to his own son and rocked him gently off to sleep.

While the previous missing children had been treated like runaways, now there was no question that somebody was abducting children in the Lower Mainland area. The media went berserk. A missing little boy, the threat of a serial murderer in their midst—it was the perfect storm as far as the newspapers and television were concerned. The ratings and paper sales were fantastic in the days that followed the child's disappearance, growing better and better as the chance of little Simon being found alive grew worse and worse.

The police immediately came under scrutiny for failing to connect the previous disappearances, lambasted and abused by politicians and press alike. The missing persons cases were passed to homicide detectives, and a whole new investigation began. An investigation that soon narrowed in on Clifford Olson as one of the potential suspects.

Clifford was entirely unaware of any of this, of course. He was entirely lost to the realities of what was going on around him. His fantasy world, where he got to indulge in all of his most vile and base desires, became his whole world. He went through the motions of his normal day-to-day life in a daydream, all of his thoughts turned towards the next time that he would be free to run wild.

He managed a full week before he killed again on the ninth—far less time than between his previous victims, but far more time than between those still to come.

Judy Kozma was a fourteen-year-old girl with far better prospects than most of the victims that Clifford had selected before. Either he had grown so confident in his ability to avoid the police that he no longer cared if his victims had families who would swiftly report their absence, or he was becoming sloppy. Given that he seemed to be slipping more and more into a kind of delirium as the killings grew more and more frequent, it seems likely that it was the latter. He picked her up in New Westminster as she was walking home from school, offering her a job at his construction company and showing off his flashy business card to her with his winning smile sparkling away as brightly as the 3D graphic he'd paid to have put on it.

He was in top form with her, talking her into the car without even breaking a sweat. She was excited about the prospect of an after-school job, just like so many of his other victims had been, but there was something about her that made her special. Some lack of reluctance that he hadn't expected, like she'd just been waiting for him to show up all this time. He went through the interview questions with her in the car, disregarding the red flag answers that usually would have made him drop her off and run away for his own safety. She'd need to call her parents when they arrived at the job site. She had people waiting at home for her who'd be wondering why she wasn't back yet. She wasn't fretting about it, exactly. It wasn't like her parents were ogres who'd be angry about her running late for a good reason, but she didn't want to worry them for no good reason.

With the interview done, Clifford offered her a celebratory drink, and buoyed along by his good humour, she took a sip. Not enough to knock her out like most of his victims, but enough to make the world seem woozy and hazy.

They kept on chatting away, even as the day dragged on and on. She realised how late it was getting, and how far they were from town, but Clifford quashed all of her concerns with the same laugh that met most of her questions. He'd straighten everything out. She didn't have to worry about a thing.

When they pulled off onto a dirt road by Weaver Lake, looping around to a side of it that he'd never visited before, her concern became fear at last. Something palpable that he could taste. He fell silent and savoured it, basking in the coming glory as she shouted and slapped at him and he felt nothing at all but pure unadulterated joy.

As he pulled the truck to a halt, she made a break for it, yanking on the door handle and setting off at a sprint back along the road towards civilisation. He laughed aloud as she went over her ankle, school shoes getting stuck in the rut in the road. Taking hold of her by her hair, he guided her back to the truck even as she flailed and screamed. She was crying for help over and over again until he drew the knife out from under her seat in the cab. Then she fell silent abruptly. It was not the only toy that he had stowed away in the truck to use that night. He drew the other one out and showed it to her.

It was a little tape recorder, the kind students or journalists used to take notes. He pressed record and held it out towards her, like he expected her to have something to say. She screamed for help, and the smile on his face could not have been wider.

He tucked that away in his pocket and led her by the throat off into the deep dark woods, down towards the lake and the soft ground on which he'd take her and bury her. This time, his crimes had a silent witness. The recorder. He wanted to relive the things he was doing in the times when he couldn't be doing them. He wanted to come back to these precious moments over and over again. Fist striking flesh. Groans. Moans. His own bestial grunts. The scintillating sound of a knife point dragged over bare skin. The wet sound as it plunged inside, again and again. All of it was good. All of it was exciting. But the best parts, the very best parts that he listened to, locked in his bathroom, towel stuffed into the crack beneath the door to muffle all sound, was the screaming.

Usually, he didn't allow screaming. He didn't like the risk, the increased chances of being overheard or interrupted. The calculating part of his brain shied away from it, but the animal part that craved all the murder and mayhem that he wrought longed for those sounds. He had made an exception for Judy, because he wanted this recording.

The first time that he listened to it, it felt as good as having her there in the flesh again. The second time, the immediacy of the memory had faded. By the third, fourth and fifth times, there wasn't enough to get him off properly. It was the skulking around, he decided. Out in the open air, he felt everything, but now he had to hide and sneak and cover up for himself. He detested it. Why shouldn't everyone in the world see what he'd done? Hear what he'd done?

The newspapers made the connection between Judy and the other missing kids as fast as the police did. They were out interviewing her sobbing parents the same day that she was reported missing, taking pictures of them outside of her house, publishing every detail that might have helped make a connection in someone's mind.

One of Clifford's friends from work had seen the girl on the night that she went missing. He had seen her in Clifford's truck. Or at least, he thought he had. He rang it into the police, readily admitting that he couldn't say for sure and that he didn't want to go on record. It was another straw in the haystack of their investigation, another nudge in the right direction that they simply did not have time to follow up on in the midst of all the other calls.

The problem with all of the information about Judy's family being available to the public was that Clifford was a part of the public. From the address, he found the phone number of the owner, and with that number he called them up and mocked them. He spoke about Judy's final moments. How she sobbed and begged and bled. He played a recording of her screams down the phone.

If her parents had been on the other end of the line, it would have been a nightmarish torment like no other. Fortunately, Clifford's detective work left a lot to be desired. He didn't find the phone number of the Kozma house. He found the phone number of the owner of the Kozma house, ringing up their landlord and playing his foul recordings to him instead.

What was said was passed along to the police—every detail of the recording, too—and a tap was put on his phone so that any future calls could be recorded, but there was no way of knowing who had made the call, or from where. Still, it put to bed the idea that the missing children were runaways, kidnapping victims, or unrelated deaths. There could be no question now that there was a sadist preying on the children of British Columbia.

 That same sadist realised that he may have overplayed his hand with the recordings. For all of his other myriad flaws, Clifford was not stupid. He understood that he had exposed himself by sharing some part of his secret pleasure with others. And while emotionally he may have been going entirely berserk due to the lack of repercussions, logically he recognised that continuing as he was would end in his incarceration.

The two lives that he lived pulled him in opposite directions, and for a time he was safe in that ambivalence. He could not act one way or the other with his emotions and mind in such opposition to one another, and so days went by when he did nothing at all. The mask of sanity stayed fixed in place; he went through the routine of daily life. Kissing his wife on the cheek before heading out to work. Rocking his son to sleep before laying him in his cot. Living his life like he was a perfectly normal human being—when nothing could be further from the truth.

The struggle inside of him went back and forth, with either side gaining the upper hand in turn with the rise and fall of the sun. By night all of his dark desires built until he felt like he would lose his mind, but in the light of day rationality won out, crushing everything down again. Not destroying it but compacting it until it was denser and more potent.

It should come as no surprise which side of him won out in the end.

Raymond King Junior was fifteen years old when Clifford picked him up in New Westminster. The boy was out on a job hunt at the time, and Clifford just so happened to cross his path. He switched gears into his smooth-talking spiel without a pause for breath, offering up work on a job site and flashing his business card before the kid even had the chance to think twice. The boy was stockier than the other ones that Clifford had preyed on. Almost as big as a man. When he took the celebratory drink with his new boss, the drugs didn't affect him nearly as strongly as Clifford might have hoped. On the way to Weaver Lake, he seemed to realise that something was wrong, the haze of the drugs finally giving way to understanding that he had been doped. Like Judy, he tried to make a break for it. Unlike Judy, he was drugged heavily enough that he didn't wait for the moving truck to stop before yanking on the door handle and leaping clear.

Clifford slammed on the breaks of the truck and leapt out with the engine still idling. All his fatherly pretences had fallen away, the jolly demeanour replaced with a dead stare as he marched around the back of his truck and after the boy where he'd fled to the side of the road.

With the drugs in his system, Raymond hadn't gotten far, but his thinking was beginning to lose its fogginess as adrenaline flooded his body. He was sober enough to understand that the drugs were in his system, interfering with his every movement, but not sober enough to do anything about it. He didn't dare run along the rocky road for fear of tripping, and there was no way he was going to get past Clifford, who now loomed huge and terrifying between him and the truck. There was no escape.

For his part, Clifford had no intention of screwing around either. His murderous passions had been in conflict with a fear of something just like this happening, and he had absolutely no intention of giving this boy even a momentary chance of ruining his life.

He caught the boy by the shoulders, hefted him like a sack and flung him off the road down the embankment. Raymond tumbled end over end, hitting the rocks head-first then rolling down to be ripped up by every jagged stone between the road and the bottom. He lay in a tangled heap at the bottom of the slope, dazed and bleeding and broken, but alive.

The tree line was not far from where he'd landed. He could feel the bones in his leg were broken, but if he could get out of sight, maybe he could hide. He started to crawl away, dragging himself over the rough ground, opening up his existing wounds and scratching new ones into his flesh.

Clifford skidded down the slope to stand over him. All the man's lumbering clumsiness vanished as his true nature asserted itself. This Clifford was not comedically oversized—he was just a huge, strong man. He caught Raymond by the belt and dragged him back, hands shaking with rage.

Raymond managed to roll himself over and look the man in the eye as he crouched down, but any compassion he had hoped he might invoke was absent from that face. Clifford scooped up a rock in his hand and brought it down.

There was no time to play. No time for fun. This had to end fast. Anyone driving along the road would see his abandoned truck. They'd stop and look down. He couldn't have that. The roads out here were rarely travelled so late, but he was not going to trust in luck to keep him out of jail.

The rock rose, and the rock slammed down. Over and over again. Smashing through the boy's face. Through his skull. Through his brain. Over and over until all that was left of the child was a thick dribbling mush on the stones beneath him.

Clifford was covered in his blood, but it didn't matter. He had cleaning supplies up in the truck. With another contemptuous heave, he tossed what was left of the boy's body into the trees and climbed back up to the road.

That brush with danger should have crushed his impulsive murdering side back down, but instead, it made things worse. Rather than being scared off by the near miss, instead, he was furious that his desires had been thwarted yet again as well as by the need to remain hidden. It sickened him, and the angrier that he got, the closer death drew for another innocent person.

The next day, he was out again on the hunt. Sigrun Arnd was a travelling student visiting Canada from Germany. She had only arrived in Coquitlam a few hours before Clifford spotted her by the roadside and offered to give her a ride. She was older than the other girls he had preyed on, eighteen and away from her family for the first time. Nobody knew exactly where she was, not even her. She was enjoying her wandering and the boundless hospitality of the Canadians that she had met. By the point that Clifford came along, she was convinced that everyone in the country was kind and helpful. When he offered her a lift, and even a tour of some local landmarks, she thought that it was par for the course with all of the other lovely people she had met so far.

He even offered her a drink, since it was a warm day, and while she wasn't usually a fan of alcohol, she wanted to be polite to her host and knocked it back quite readily.

The same pattern as had played out so many times before, followed. He raped her while the drugs still held her defenceless, and then he drew out his hammer and began methodically beating her, finishing up with lethal blows to the skull. Where before he had dug graves for his victims, the frenzy that was driving him that day left no time for such civilised pursuits. He tossed her body into a water-filled ditch out by the river in

Richmond and thought no more about it. None of this mattered. He was invincible. He had spent so much time cowering and sneaking around when there was no need at all. He had killed a boy with a rock the night before; there was no need to get clever about things. He wasn't untouchable because he was clever.

It was about this time that the police began to focus their investigation in on Clifford. Most still didn't entertain the thought that he was the perpetrator, but they thought he might well be a valuable source of information. With the new sexual assault charge against him still pending, they had leverage, and they meant to use it.

Bringing him in for questioning once more, the police asked him extensively about the missing children and anything he knew about new criminals in the area who might be responsible. Sensing a lucrative opportunity to turn his knowledge of the situation to his advantage for once, Clifford immediately asked how much they'd be willing to pay for intelligence. The police went back and forth over what discretionary funds might be available to tip their informant, but unless they could be certain that whatever Clifford had to say would lead to an arrest, they didn't know what they could swing.

As for Clifford, he obviously wasn't prepared to throw himself into jail for some cash when the police had nothing on him. His head was spinning trying to come up with the best way to profit from the situation without incriminating himself. He attempted to avoid connecting himself to the crimes that ended up tipping off the police to his direct involvement. Instead of offering to find the perpetrator, he suggested to them that he could find the bodies of the victims for them, guiding them to the secret places that they'd been hidden in exchange for lump sums of cash.

It was information that could not have been acquired through the grapevine, but something that only the perpetrator or an accomplice would know about. Clifford went from being one of a dozen potential sources to somebody that was guaranteed to have direct contact with their killer. The police made excuses, claiming any money paid out would have to come from the political side of things, and then cut him loose while they made enquiries about what the local prosecutors might be willing to pay for bodies.

The plan was never to pay him. Instead, Clifford was immediately placed under surveillance. Throughout the day, the police would track him as he went about his business until he returned home, on the assumption that he was just the small-time ex-con that he appeared to be and would be making any contact with the killer during those daylight hours.

It was a mistake that would prove fatal.

Retracing his steps and reliving his kills, Clifford returned to the motor court where Christine Weller had lived and spotted another victim just waiting for his loving ministrations. Fifteen-year-old Terri Lynn Carson lived in an apartment complex right next door, and while Clifford didn't immediately swoop in to abduct her, he did keep a casual eye on the girl each time that he passed. Eventually, he spotted her heading away from home and finally intercepted her on 108th Avenue, where she was patiently waiting for her bus to arrive. His usual routine was curbed in favour of simply offering the girl a lift. It was three days since he'd last satisfied himself with the unfortunate German tourist, and the need was rising sharply within him. If it wasn't Terri, then it would have been some other girl. She just happened to be the unfortunate one that his eye had stopped on. Once he had her in the car, he plied her with drink, just as he had so many before her, and once she was insensible, he drove out in a remote area out east of Chilliwack to seal the deal.

He raped her as he had the ones before, while the drugs in her system still had her insensible, but then he waited and waited as realisation and panic crept back into her features. He waited until she had the wherewithal to draw in a lungful of breath and scream, then, before the sound could escape, he clamped his meaty hands around her throat and squeezed.

Most of his victims had died from acts of truly horrific violence. Brutal stabbings and beatings. The kind of thing that only a wild animal in human skin could inflict. Poor Terri was different. The way that he killed her was almost gentle by comparison, intimate, as he stared into her eyes and choked the life out of her as she flailed. In his mind, he was reliving his first kill all over again, trying to recapture the impossible high he'd felt when he started down this awful road. This was the same girl, in his head, the same girl from the same dead end, who he could do anything to and never suffer any consequences. He could take his time this time. He could do it right.

It was almost enough to feel as good as the first time. Almost.

Once again, he fell into the same fugue state, going through his daily life like he was on automatic pilot as he lived and relived all of his sordid acts in fantasy. Letting the hunger build again. Normally when a serial killer enters a berserk phase like he was experiencing in that month, the breakdown of their organisation that ensues results in their early capture, but there was no real change to Clifford's patterns of behaviour. That same balance of passion and calculation persisted, as though he were on autopilot when it came to concealing his crimes as much as fixing blocked sinks or teaching his son how to walk. Three days had passed between each of his previous killings, and three days after Terri's death, he killed again.

Louise Chartrand was a little older than his usual victims at the age of seventeen. She was on her way to work in Maple Ridge, British Columbia, when he pulled alongside her and offered her a ride the rest of the way. Even with all of the stories of dead girls circulating, it did not cross Louise's mind that the charming middle-aged man offering her a lift to work might be the monster behind the crime spree. Still, she wasn't entirely without her wits. As they rode along, she noted early when he seemed to be heading away from her work, and her sense of responsibility led her to turn down the offer of liquor.

When things were clearly taking a turn for the worse, she tried to talk her way out of the situation, then reached for the doorhandle despite the speed that they were moving at. Clifford was not willing to take any risks. In one motion, he scooped the hammer from beneath his seat and struck her on the temple. She was out cold before he made another swing.

He continued on the road out of town and up Whistler Mountain, where he unloaded the still-breathing body of Louise and inflicted all of his usual horrors upon her. If such things satisfied him, it barely showed anymore. It was no longer enough. Even killing day after day was not enough to satisfy his urges. The moment that he had buried her body he was back on the road again. Back on the hunt.

Deal With the Devil

In one month, Clifford had killed as many children and teenagers as he had in his whole life before that—a bloody frenzy that could not escape notice of the police hunting for their serial killer. Despite having Clifford under sporadic surveillance after his attempt to sell them information only the killer would know, there was very little belief that the man was actually behind the killings. Nothing in his record suggested the kind of violence involved, and nobody could get their heads around the idea that this small-time nobody might actually be a prolific serial killer. Most of the already taxed investigation considered him to be a dead lead that was eating up valuable manpower, a waste of time when there were so many serious offenders out there who fit their profile so much better.

The task force officers observed him committing a variety of lesser crimes in their time with eyes on him, including a pair of lucrative burglaries. It was of no surprise to them, given his history, and it explained where his income was coming from when his business ventures were clearly just for show. It was of little interest to them. They let him walk free without even questioning him. They had much bigger fish to fry than some petty criminal breaking into houses.

Yet there were still some lower ranking officers who stuck to Clifford despite the general disinterest in him—men who considered the possibility that his offer was legitimate, and that he might have encountered the killer in his journeys through the criminal underworld. Those same officers reported back to their superiors, day after day, that they had not observed him making contact with any of the potential suspects, as they'd been asked, but they also began drawing some conclusions of their own, watching him.

His erratic behaviour, drug use, and Jekyll and Hyde mannerism switches when he thought that he was not being observed all concerned the observers, and gradually they began to consider the very real possibility that he was, in fact, the killer that they were waiting for him to meet. Even when they were not scheduled to be watching him, the officers began ensuring that one of their little team was keeping an eye on his activities, and while their coverage was not perfect, it did mean that more and more of his behaviour was observed, ever increasing their suspicion, even though the exact moments that he struck managed to go unobserved.

That would change all too quickly.

Clifford was going about business as usual, completely unaware of the police tailing him as he went about that business. There was never really any pattern to his behaviour, not even when he wasn't up to anything suspicious. He seemed to travel almost at random around the local area, driving for hours, talking to anyone he met but never making contact lasting beyond that. It was like he was in his own world. During these drives, he was observed drinking and popping pills, but they didn't seem to make any difference to him. He didn't change with them. Whatever altered state he was in, it was too deep for booze or drugs to touch.

These rambling trips were considered to be the biggest waste of resources and time by the higher ups in the police department, given how long these jaunts lasted and how much ground he managed to cover. In fuel costs alone, Clifford was costing the police a small fortune. But that fateful day in August, it finally paid off.

He had been trawling back and forth over Vancouver Island for hours by the time that he drew up to a pair of hitchhikers at the side of the road in Ucluelet. From their unmarked car, the police could see everything. He wound down his window and leaned out to chat with the girls. Both of them teenagers. Both of them a perfect fit for the serial killer's preferred victim type.

What had been a routine, dull trip suddenly became the tensest moment in the young officers' lives. They sat back, watching as he talked to the girls slowly, calmly, almost disinterested, like he didn't care whether they took a ride with him or not. It was just like every other time he'd pulled up for a chat through the day. Completely normal and fine—unless he was the killer.

If he was the killer, then the police were watching him abduct his latest victims. The moment that they were in his car, literally anything might happen to them, and the officers watching would have to spend the rest of their lives sickened by the knowledge that they could have intervened. They could have saved those girls' lives.

As the conversation stretched on and on, panic in the police car began to mount. They argued back and forth, citing the evidence they'd gathered. Trying frantically to piece everything together. To prove to themselves that Clifford was not the serial killer. Back and forth they went, citing evidence and countering it with the next word, neither officer truly certain, but both of them overcome with dread that their inaction might result in the death of two innocent girls. The decision was taken out of their hands a moment later when the girls walked around to climb up into the truck's cabin—the moment of truth, when the investigators had to decide whether they bungle their investigation for the safety of the public or they let things play out so that they could get the evidence that they needed. As Clifford Olson pulled away with those girls in his truck, humanity won out.

Whipping out a siren, the unmarked car pulled the truck over. The officers extracted the girls from Clifford's truck while he acted lost and confused; then, in a brief moment of brilliance, the shadowing cops arrested him for the burglaries that they knew he had committed. It was obvious to everyone involved that it was the safety of the girls that the arresting officers cared about, given the trouble they went to arranging for a car to come out and drive them to safety.

Any hope of catching him in the act was ruined. Any hope of following him to the killer was ruined. The long-running and expensive observation of Clifford came to an ignominious end. He was consigned to a cell in Burnaby on the burglary charges with no hope of bail given his long history of escape attempts. It was then that the higher-ranking officers of the serial killer investigation stepped in, still not believing that Clifford was the party responsible but hoping to parlay his latest arrest into the kind of leverage that might make him give up more information on the killer if he had it.

They went in fully expecting him to roll over the same way that he always did to avoid jail time, but the man they had in that jail cell was not the Clifford that they were accustomed to dealing with. The charm was still there, but all of the feigned fear and weakness seemed to have vanished. He offered them a deal: he'd guide them to the bodies if they paid him cash. Put into trust for his wife and kid, of course. When asked what he thought the value of that information might be, he replied $10,000 per body. The police thought that this whole thing was laughable, some sort of scam. Once more, however, the younger officers involved in the case pushed the idea that Clifford might be their perpetrator. His odd behaviour in interrogation was just enough to convince the interviewing officers that something was off kilter with the man, even if they weren't ready to believe that he was their killer, so they gave the go-ahead, and suddenly the task force moved into action the way that it should have from the moment Clifford was picked up.

Starting with his truck, forensics scoured for evidence. Almost immediately they discovered his little box of toys:—the syringes, drugs, and weapons that he'd used to conduct his awful business—but they were all clean, showing no signs of any illegal use. Yet every new item they uncovered added another layer of suspicion. Every inch of the car was gone over with a fine-toothed comb, searching for any evidence of the previous victims, or even anything that might tie Clifford to the areas where they'd been abducted at the time. Parking tickets, receipts, anything that they could use to place him. Yet for all his appearance of utter carelessness, there was a streak of organisation to Clifford that wasn't immediately apparent. When he entered the fugue state that ruled him while he was killing, he seemed to become hyper-aware of anything that might be used against him at a later date. He had disposed of absolutely everything.

Everything except for a notebook that the investigators found wedged underneath the passenger side seat, so far back it was jamming up the mechanism for adjusting the seat's position: a school notebook with the name Judy Kozma written on the cover, in her handwriting.

The interrogation ground to a complete halt. The course of the investigation had entirely changed. This was no longer a peripheral issue bothering the task force—this had just become the primary focus for the entire investigation. The original interrogators were traded off for the lead detectives, who were rapidly briefed on a man who they hadn't so much as looked at since the initial disappearance that kicked off the summer of terror.

They talked back and forth for hours on end, having to send out food and cigars for Clifford multiple times to keep the conversation going. By the end of the back and forth, everyone in the task force was convinced that Olson was the perpetrator, just from his offhand references to things that the general public would not have been privy to. He was the killer that they were looking for.

And they had nothing.

There was one piece of material evidence tying Clifford to the crime. Even if the case were to make it to court, any sane judge would throw it away. Worse yet, even if they managed to extract a confession from the wily man happily puffing away in the interrogation room, the court would not consider it admissible unless there was something to back it up. This was not the Wild West, where a man's word was all it took to clear cases off the book. They needed hard evidence to put a man away for murder. Otherwise, coerced confessions would be the order of the day.

The police took what they had from the interrogation to the provincial prosecutors, offering up all the various pieces of circumstantial evidence they'd pulled together about Clifford, including all of the information that he'd let slip during his interrogation, but it still wasn't enough. It wouldn't hold up in court. They had the serial killer in custody, and he was going to walk away scot-free if they didn't get proof.

At this point, the police only had four bodies, and nothing tying Clifford to any of them. Frantic searches of his house had turned up nothing. Interrogating his wife had turned up nothing.

Corporal Fred Maile went back into the room alone with him to negotiate a deal. He was the only man with the stomach for it. The tone of things changed entirely. This was no longer an attempt to trick or coerce information out of an unwilling interviewee; this was a business meeting where both sides were seeking satisfaction.

'Eleven bodies for $100,000,' came Clifford's first offer.

Maile repeated it back to him carefully. 'For $100,000 in cash, you will provide us with the bodies of the missing kids.'

'And a statement on each one. Evidence, keepsakes from the bodies, stuff that only the killer would have. I'll sign off on each one.'

Maile's eyes narrowed. 'Well listen, we'd have to work something out. We can't just give you all that money on your say-so. We'd need some sort of assurances that you're on the level.'

'Likewise. I want to make sure my Joan is getting the money before we go any further, make sure this isn't some sort of trick. So, I figure what we'll do is I'll give you a freebie up front. I'll give you a body and a statement. You'll have the 10 thousand in cash, and when we're done at the scene, you'll call your man and he'll hand that over to my Joanie. Then I'll call Joan, make sure she's got it. And you call your man. Then we can roll on to the rest.'

It was a well formulated plan, carefully calculated. If nothing else, the level of depth and planning that had gone into it convinced any police watching that this might actually be the organised serial killer they'd been stalking instead of the clumsy oaf they'd seen in the past.

Still, Maile wasn't willing to just go along with anything this criminal said without some pushback. His brow furrowed as he tried to work through any flaws in this plan—other than the obvious career suicide if news of this deal ever came out.

'What about your lawyer? You think he's just going to sit back and let his client go down for all these murders?'

'My lawyer?' Clifford smirked. 'He works for me. He'll do what I tell him to do.'

Clifford announced that they needed a contract, and since his hands were still cuffed, he had no option but to dictate it to Maile, who scrawled it out on some blank paper.

'This is an undertaking of an agreement between the RCMP and Clifford Robert Olson. The following will be paid by the RCMP to Mrs. Joan Olson for the following information: $10,000 cash for each body of missing persons up to seven bodies. $30,000 for information of four bodies which have already been recovered which relate to the above seven other missing persons. The agreement should be undertaken and shall be binding in law as to not disclose this information in this agreement to the Canadian Press. The following missing persons are covered in this agreement: Judy Kozma, Daryn Johnsrude, Raymond King, Simon Partington, Ada Court, Louise Chartrand, Christine Weller, Terri-Lyn Carson, Colleen Daignault and Sandra Wolfsteiner and one unidentified female. $10,000 will be paid to Mrs. Olson up to a total of the recovery of seven bodies.'

The pen was placed in Clifford's hand, and he signed his future away. As did Maile, although he was quick to point out to Clifford that any deal of this size would need to be approved by someone further up the ladder of command. He didn't have the authority to dispense that kind of money. Clifford couldn't care less. He was certain that he'd be getting his money because he had something that nobody else in the world had. Better yet, he was finally going to be able to come out of the shadows and have his magnificence seen. All these years he'd been masquerading as some petty criminal nobody. All these years the big scary murderers in prisons had looked down their noses at him. Well now they would know he was the biggest killer of them all, and soon everybody in the world was going to know it, too. He was the bogeyman, the monster under your children's bed—he was everything a parent feared.

He called his wife when the interview was over, gloating that she was going to be rich. That she was going to live in the lap of luxury thanks to the new deal he'd just cut. She was less excited about that and more concerned about the police that had been tearing up her house while he'd been missing. More than that, though, she was horrified about the questions that they'd been asking her about him. Where he'd been. What he'd been doing. If he'd been coming home late. If she'd noticed blood on his clothes when she did the laundry. In typical Clifford fashion, he'd been so caught up in the excitement of cutting the best deal of his life that he'd forgotten that she might be a tad upset with him for being a mass murderer.

Well aware that any calls he was making would be recorded, and careful not to give away any leverage too soon, he fobbed her off with a promise that he'd explain everything later, in person, and that she didn't have anything to worry about. She should expect a visit from his lawyer, who'd lay things out for her more clearly, and she should set all of her worries aside. He had seen to a bright future for her and their baby.

When Maile said that he didn't have the authority to disburse the frankly ridiculous amount of cash required to close this case once and for all, he wasn't joking. Neither he nor his commanding officers nor anyone within the police force itself had the authority to do it. The decision was passed farther and farther up the chain until finally, it reached Attorney-General Allan Williams, the man in charge of criminal justice for the whole of Canada.

Williams was not a stranger to hard decisions, or to political hot potatoes being tossed his way, but there was something fundamentally wrong with the deal that had been laid out for Olson. There has always been a degree of give and take in the criminal justice system—plea bargains and backroom deals, exchanging lesser charges for greater ones if it will ensure a guilty verdict, even the constant flow of money and dropped charges that informants like Olson had benefited from in the past. It was the oil that made the clunking machinery of policing and prosecution continue to turn. Yet there was always one fundamental rule governing every decision that was made. It must never benefit the criminal. Crime should not pay. If criminals could turn themselves in for cash pay-outs, it would be a slippery slope to the whole system collapsing.

This deal that Olson was proposing ran entirely contrary to that fundamental rule. It was rewarding a man for committing the most heinous acts imaginable. It was also the right decision, at least on paper.

Taking all morality out of the equation and looking at the numbers in front of him, the cost of keeping the investigation running for longer would easily surmount what was being asked by Olson. Not to mention the innumerable other deaths that would inevitably follow. Now that he was aware that he was under observation, it would be simple enough for a cunning criminal to work around his surveillance teams. If Olson got back on the streets, there was no question that he would kill again. So, the numbers game was no longer just about the exchange of funds for a conviction. It was about the human cost, the number of people that Williams was willing to sacrifice on the altar of his own high principles.

He had looked over all of the evidence himself, and as it stood, there was no way that they could secure a conviction. Even if they took the one 'freebie' that Olson had offered and let the rest remain unsolved, it would be a permanent blight on the record of his justice department, but more importantly, it would leave the parents of the victims in perpetual limbo, never knowing if their loved ones had fallen prey to him or not. So long as Olson had leverage, there was no way that he would give it up, and now that he had a sense for how much his information was worth, there would be no hope of prying it out of him for less. If this case was going to be closed to anyone's satisfaction, it had to be now. Not to mention the mysterious 'other body' that Olson had offered up to round out the ten. A bodiless murder without even a name attached to it was not the sort of thing that he wanted floating around out there.

There were provisions in the agreement that Olson would not disclose that he was being paid for his information, and it seemed likely that he would abide by that. It was not in his interest to disrupt the deal he had so painstakingly constructed and that benefited him so greatly. So long as the departmental police could keep their mouths shut, they might actually get away with cutting this deal while keeping all of their careers intact. If anything, closing out this serial killer case would be a feather in their caps, particularly in the eyes of the general public.

Williams signed off on the deal, but he didn't like it.

He liked it even less when Olson was paraded into his office just a few days later, blithely chatting away with his lawyers, trailed by his catatonic wife and the police officers who seemed to be mostly along for the ride. He strode about as if he owned the place, cracking jokes and grinning as he strolled into the office at the top of the Sun Tower.

Joan's lawyer leaned over to her and asked, 'Does your husband know what he's doing?'

And while she couldn't bring herself to speak, she did manage to nod. Sadly, the interaction was enough to catch Clifford's attention, and he swooped in behind his wife, still grinning away, putting his hands on her shoulders and declaring to the world, 'What can I say honey? I did it. Everything they're saying I did. It was the booze and the pills. Not me.'

The fact he couldn't keep the glee out of his voice did nothing to sell this pathetic attempt at an apology, and Joan burst into wailing and tears once more, clearly just as much a victim of Olson as anyone else.

Matters grew even more disgusting when he caught sight of the soft-sided briefcase at the side of the Attorney General's desk. He literally started rubbing his hands together.

Once more talking over everyone else in the room, he started explaining how he wanted the money disbursed: the amount to go to the lawyers for their fees, the stipend he wanted paid to his parents for old time's sake, and the rest to be put in trust for Joan and their baby boy.

As the money was counted out, he jostled his lawyer's arm with his elbow. 'You ever seen that much money before?'

He turned to his lawyer, Robert Shantz, and suggested that there was more money to be made here if he wanted to write a book about the case. 'Kiss Daddy Goodbye' was his proposed title, and he offered to give Shantz all the information that he wanted on his crime spree in exchange for a cut of the royalties. While Shantz was willing to collect his fee from Olson, it seemed that was as far as he wanted their business dealings to go. He was practically holding his nose while standing next to the odious man.

As for Williams, he later described feeling physically sick as the blood money was handed over to Olson's lawyers. He said that if Satan himself had appeared in a cloud of sulphur and brimstone he wouldn't have been surprised.

From there, the day only became more horrific and depraved. Olson was dressed up in police uniform with a cap pulled low over his face as a disguise, and then began the tour of his greatest hits. He sat in the back seat of an unmarked car with four detectives. Corporal Maile sat beside him with a recorder in hand, the microphone pointed towards Olson to record every word that came out of his mouth during their journey. Clifford was in his element as the centre of attention, revelling in the fact that everyone was hanging on his every word, delighted to be appreciated for his true self, in as much as anyone could appreciate it. If the killings had been his sex, this was the cigar afterwards. He seemed almost blissful as he recounted where he'd picked up each of his victims, how he had talked them into getting into his truck with the promise of $10 an hour work and dosed them with a chloral hydrate 'Mickey Finn' to ensure that they were too weak and disoriented to fight back against him when the time came to rape, torture, and murder them. Every detective in the car was a veteran officer, yet they were all sickened by the descriptions that Olson was providing. This wasn't the detached reports that they were accustomed to, where all the depth of detail was stripped away and sanitised for their regular consumption. This was erotica for serial killers, every gruesome detail described. Death rattles, and smells, and the twitches that could be extracted from a dead body by twisting a metal spike in the brain.

A convoy of police cars followed after that first car—officers to secure each of the eleven sites, police dogs to sniff out bodies, and the entire forensics department as would be required to search each of the dumpsites.

At the site of each dumped body, Clifford would get out of the car, walk to the exact spot where the dead body could be found, and then re-enact the killing. Pantomiming his actions, describing his victim's struggles and providing the police with every detail that they needed to convict him. His memory of the murders was encyclopaedic; not once did he lead them astray. It was as though the moments when he was killing had burned themselves permanently into his mind, an immovable object in a world that was otherwise in constant flux for him. Who he was changed from moment to moment as he presented whatever face he thought his audience wanted to see. None of it felt real to him, but this felt real: when the mask was off and he could do what he wanted, be who he wanted to be, above petty ideas like popularity or morality. Here he had perfect clarity.

Each body was exhumed, the site secured, and Olson's confession completely recorded before a call was made to his lawyer to transfer the money over to Joan's bank account. It was the most profitable day of Clifford's life, and despite clearly revelling in the experience of being at the centre of attention, he seemed to be constantly pacing, desperate to move on to the next site and bank more money.

As it turned out, without Olson's presence it was entirely likely that the bodies would never have been uncovered. Even if they had, the condition that the decaying corpses had progressed to meant that most would have been beyond identification. One was mummified by the time it was extracted from the peat-heavy soil. Another could only be identified from dental records. It took pathologists to identify the majority of them. Coming upon the remains of German tourist Sigrun Arnd, the unidentified body of an unknown victim, the police realised that she would never have even been missed were it not for Clifford's confessions. She would have vanished without a trace. Even with her body and his description of her, it took months to retrieve official records of her so that her death could be properly certified.

Throughout all of this, Clifford was happily puffing away on his cigars and cracking jokes with the police as though they were his co-workers. The way he saw it, they were. He put the bodies in the ground, they dug them up, like a farmer planting and harvesting a crop. To his reasoning, this was all good news for the police, too. Their clearance record was about to skyrocket. They should have loved him.

The detectives who had to ride with him, listening to his appalling descriptions of death and destruction, were not taken in by his joviality, but the other police in the convoy found the charismatic monster too charming to resist. When it came around to mealtimes, they were the ones who'd take Olson to a steakhouse where he'd happily guzzle down colas, thick sirloins, and baked potatoes while they all chatted convivially.

He was living the high life, with only hard liquor and his usual drugs denied to him. He could get used to that kind of treatment.

As they drove from crime scene to crime scene, the endless parade of death didn't stop. Even when Clifford was silent, the radio crackled and chattered away with hourly reports in the local press about the recovery of bodies on each day. When that was silent, there was the internal police radio, where reports were being passed back and forth from pathologists and crime scene investigators uncovering each gruesome detail of the killings exactly as Olson had described it, right down to the pattern of blows with his 'silver hammer' or the invisible death that caused an embolism. For Clifford it was all good news. It all verified that what he was saying was the truth, and the truth was certain to be rewarded. Body by body, the deposits were made into Joan's account until finally, days after the horrific parade had begun, it was finally over. She was $100,000 richer, and the police had eleven murders that they could mark as solved.

He'd been returned to the police station to wait out the veritable tidal wave of paperwork that his day's work had generated when he demanded another meeting with Corporal Maile. Until that moment, everything had been going according to plan. Smoother than anticipated even, since the Attorney General had called in a metric ton of favours to control the media's reporting on the matter. In exchange for a steady flow of information from the justice department, the press would not push their luck by looking into the case any further than was necessary. Given the depth of detail that was being 'leaked' to them throughout the first few days, it was hardly surprising that the Canadian press were in no rush to go digging—they'd scarcely have time to report anything more than they already had. There was only so much space in the newspaper and so many hours of television to fill in a day. Any more than they'd already received would have overflowed the margins.

Maile came running to Olson's beck and call, dreading the inevitable twist when the killer slipped through his fingers or stabbed him in the back. That was not what Clifford had in mind. He was more than satisfied with how things had shaken out in the end. He had his money, he had his legacy, everything was coming up Olson. No. What he wanted was to cut another deal.

He knew the police had him now. He'd be going to jail and serving his time. There was no way that he was ever going to see the light of day again after all he'd confessed to. But that didn't mean that he couldn't make their job easier and pocket some more cash for Joan and his kid.

He'd given them the first taste for free. They'd been willing to pay $100,000 for just ten bodies. $10,000 a pop. Now he was offering them a bulk-buy discount. He was willing to slash his price to $5,000 a body for the next twenty solved murders.

Maile was gobsmacked. Not only at the offer, but at the idea that Clifford might have killed not eleven people, but thirty-one. He took a note of the deal and explained as politely as he could muster that he would need to take the deal to his superiors and let them make the call.

What had been an open and shut case suddenly spun back to life. The bodies that they had recovered almost all tied to a missing person case that had been connected with their mysterious killer, almost as though Olson, in constant contact with the police and being questioned about the missing, had given them exactly what they already thought that he was responsible for, plus the one extra, unknown, body to cover the gap that giving them the freebie at the beginning of the deal had created in his list.

There was a very real possibility that Olson had killed twenty more people. His pattern had never been consistent. His victim selection had always been on the random side. There were more than enough missing people to account for these extra victims in the areas that he was already known to hunt, and if he had only been reporting some of his crimes, then it stood to reason that he'd only give away some of his hunting grounds, too. When he was being tailed, he had certainly spent time slowly driving through areas that were not considered to be his hunting grounds. The police scrabbled to pull together all the information on missing people from those areas, hauling up cold cases, too. Trying to work out not only if Olson had truly been as prolific as he claimed, but whether it was possible that more cases had slipped through their hunt.

Pamela Lorraine Darlington had been found stripped, raped, and sexually mutilated, floating face down in the Thompson River in Kamloops, British Columbia, in November of 1973. Originally, she had been linked to Clifford's spree of killings, but the fact that she was older than his usual victims had eventually seen her removed from the hunt for that particular serial killer. Instead, it had been assumed that she was a victim of a second murderer, the supposed 'Highway Killer' responsible for the deaths of fourteen hitchhiking women picked up across the Canadian Rockies between 1972 and 1981 on the Yellowhead highway, or the tributary roads that led to it. The fact that these victims' bodies were recovered had suggested to the police that, despite the sexual assault associated with Olson's usual murders, these were the work of a different murderer. The fifteenth victim of this supposed killer, Monica Jack, went missing without a trace while bicycling the country roads near to the Yellowhead. She was twelve years old, exactly matched Olson's usual victim profile, and her body was never recovered.

This cluster of killings was only a fraction of what it now seemed possible had been the work of Clifford Olson Junior. Seventeen young women and six girls murdered between the highway of Kamloops and Banff also fit in with his usual patterns of behaviour.

Verna Bjerky was a 17-year-old waitress from the tiny community of Yale, BC, who vanished without a trace after a late evening shift waiting tables at 'Godfather' steak and pizza restaurant in nearby Hope, BC. Most nights she was working too late for bus service, so she would stay with a friend rather than fork over the fifteen dollar taxi fare to take her back to Yale, but on occasion she got lucky and she was able to hitchhike in the right direction. On the night she vanished, she was not lucky.

Despite the entire community mobilising to try and find her, she remained completely lost until October of 1981, when some of her personal effects were found scattered three miles down the highway from Hope, at the turn-off to the wilderness where Olson had taken many of his victims to finish them off and bury them. Hope was one of his regular stops when he was taking his long drives, and police had seen him eating at Godfather when he stopped there for dinner.

Mary Ellen Jamieson went missing on August 7, 1980, last seen hitchhiking on Highway 101 at Davis Bay on Vancouver Island—another area that was not officially considered part of Olson's hunting grounds, but which had been the area where he'd first been picked up with two hitchhikers in the car. She had been out for dinner with her boyfriend, but neither of them had a car, so she would have been looking to avoid a cab fare, too. Her body was discovered by a family friend out searching for her just nine days later, buried in a shallow grave off the side of a logging road, exactly the kind of area where Clifford dumped other bodies. The reason she was never connected to Clifford's spree was that she was recovered fully clothed, although her body did have a pattern of bruises around her neck. Slotting her into place with his other victims, this would have been during the period when Clifford was killing his victims by strangulation.

To Maile's mounting horror, it became apparent that Olson almost certainly had the information that they needed to close all of those cases. So many murders, committed during the time when Olson was at his most active, that they could not confirm were his unless he gave up the information. With no other choice, the corporal took the request for funds up the ladder.

The buck stopped almost immediately the moment that Maile spoke to his superiors. After the first deal had been signed, a directive had come down from Williams that no further cash deals were to be offered to Olson under any circumstances. The gist was that they had gotten lucky with this first round of victims, and the justice department had no intention of rolling the dice again. Williams had already burned through a fair portion of his clout keeping the original deal under wraps, and he had no intention of a repeat performance when the whole thing could turn into a fiasco at a moment's notice. He had his win, and he was taking it to the bank.

So Maile returned to the negotiating table with nothing in hand, forced to essentially beg Olson to give up his information as the other man became increasingly belligerent at the lack of a proper offer. He felt like he'd been exceptionally generous in the deal that he had offered to the police, given that they'd already established the value of bodies at $10,000 a pop. To be turned down felt to Olson like the police biting the hand that fed them. He was angry, but as usual, he buried it deep and smiled at the officers, telling them that the bodies would still be there when they came around. It wasn't like he was going to be going anywhere, either. They'd always know where to find him.

The Game Goes On

Pending trial, Olson was confined to jail in the general population. But his experience behind bars this time around was entirely different. No longer could he blend into the background and serve out his time in peace. The other prisoners would throw lit cigarettes at him when he passed. They tossed trash into his cell while he was sleeping. He was pushed and shoved around until finally he ended up confined to a solitary confinement cell for all but two hours a day for his own protection. One hour was used for exercise in the yard when there was nobody else about. The other hour he seemed to dedicate to making himself front page news everywhere he could. He rang local reporters and complained about the conditions that he was living in, sleeping on the floor with no running water and no lights. Living like a dog, as he described it. He was also extremely offended to discover that the suit that he had been wearing when he was brought into custody had been divested of its buttons, and that some kind soul had written 'baby-fucker' on his shirt, to jog his memory as to why he was in confinement. 'That suit cost me $200!' he complained to anyone who would listen. 'And the shirt $60! I don't have to put up with this shit. I think I should have fair treatment from the press, and I should be segregated from other inmates.'

While his constant complaints and incessant whining landed him on the front page of papers across Canada, along with the lurid details of all of his crimes, the story of his deal with the justice department remained out of the public eye. This was particularly interesting because Clifford had realised that the justice department's refusal to cut him a second deal was because they were frightened about it increasing the chances of his first deal becoming public knowledge. To remove such concerns from the equation, Olson decided that the best course to getting his second pay-out from the police was to make their first deal public knowledge. Every time that he made contact with the press, he would regale them with details of the arrangements that he had made and that would lead to his conviction. Yet they printed none of it. Despite the cash for corpses deal being the story of a lifetime, the local news placed loyalty to Williams above it.

Those that couldn't be won with the promise of favours were faced with the threat that they might be found in contempt of court if they were to print information about the deal. There was no way that knowledge of the deal would not be considered prejudicial to any jury involved in Olson's trial. Any news outlet that poisoned the jury pool would invariably have to face charges, fines, and worse. And that wasn't even taking into account the fact that it would result in a mistrial and a notorious murderer walking free to kill again.

Even when details of the deal reached the House of Commons and went up for debate, the usual broadcasting of events was censored. The families of the victims who should now have been at peace were instead confronted with conflicting stories when they begged questions of the police—like they were trying to obfuscate the story of how they'd caught a notorious serial killer instead of bragging about it. Suspicions began to mount about some sort of cover up.

The date for Olson's trial was set, but no jury was ultimately called. He elected to go along with the spirit of his original agreement with the justice department and conceded his guilt. He even managed to squeeze out some credible-looking tears as he confessed to his crimes publicly for the first time. After the court clerk read out each of the eleven first-degree murder charges against him, he hoarsely replied, 'Guilty.'

Justice Harry McKay was presiding, and during sentencing, he had a great deal to say about Clifford Olson Junior. 'No punishment that any civilised country could impose would be adequate for the severity of your crimes. You should never be granted parole for the remainder of your days. It would be foolhardy to let you at large.'

The moment that he was out of sight of the court and cameras, the crocodile tears stopped flowing and he went back to his usual jocular demeanour. When asked what he thought about the ruling that he should never have parole, he seemed pretty accepting, confiding to the officer escorting him that if he were ever set free, he'd probably pick up where he left off.

He was confined to Kingston Penitentiary, where he would spend the rest of his natural life, and for one moment it seemed that the circus surrounding him would finally come to an end. But then news of his deal was published.

With one press outlet publishing details of the cash for corpses deal, now that the risk of prosecution for interfering with the trial was past, all of the others considered their obligation to Williams expired, too. After all, the cat was already out of the bag, and it would seem even more suspicious if they did not report on what had occurred.

Understandably, both the victim's families and the public were outraged. A campaign was immediately kicked off demanding the return of the money. Or for the money to be disbursed to the families of Olson's victims, but Joan was not willing to give up her livelihood so readily.

Williams was raked over the coals in the press, and it was only a few days before he was forced to make a public statement and launch an inquiry into how his department had handled the case. 'I consider this case unique. I do not expect anything like this to occur again. The decision was not an easy one for me or the RCMP to make. It is the practice for monies to be extended in a variety of ways to obtain information, to protect witnesses, sometimes to protect others who may be associated with crimes. This matter is an extension of that principle, one that I don't expect to see repeated. The crimes were so horrible they should not be revealed. It adds nothing to dwell on details of that kind.' Despite this backpedalling and attempts to shut further inquiry down, the public demands for justice just grew louder and louder. Even Robert Shantz, Olson's lawyer, decried the decision as improper and 'politically insane'. Members of Parliament condemned the decision, and William's political career was over on the spot, but that did nothing to resolve the victims' families' feelings that this was just salt in the wound.

The police attempted to seize the money that had been paid into Joan's account but quickly discovered that it was no longer there. Despite Shantz's disdain for his client and the whole situation, he had still performed his duties as counsel to the best of his abilities, arranging for the money to be transferred overseas to prevent exactly this kind of knee-jerk reaction from the Canadian police. They raged and they fumed, but they were impotent thanks to his careful arrangements.

The public inquiry began into the chain of events that led up to the radical decision, but despite a massive press campaign to find evidence of wrongdoing, the police, justice department, and coroners all closed ranks and essentially stated that the right decision had been made. The locations where the bodies had been dumped would never have been found without the assistance of the killer. The choice not to pursue Olson from the beginning even though he was flagged up so early in the investigation was the correct one as it had seemed like he was not a viable lead. An assortment of recommendations were made to prevent history from repeating, like ensuring better surveillance coverage on anyone linked to a serial murder case, but beyond that, the police washed their hands clean of any wrongdoing.

At the same time, Joan was being harangued by the press and public for accepting the money that her husband had bequeathed to her and was forced into hiding. In a few rare interviews, she similarly absolved herself of all guilt. 'I am a good person. I can look myself in the eye in the mirror and not feel ashamed.' It was easy to view her as a victim of Olson's machinations as much as anyone, but even as she proceeded with her divorce and a change of name, the families of the victims were working their way up the ladder of courts, demanding that the decision be overturned. Yet even in the Supreme Court, they discovered that they had no legal standing. The contract that had been drawn up for Olson was airtight. Just because it was immoral, did not mean it was illegal, so the courts could offer no redress.

Of course, throughout all of this, Olson was not willing to sit back and take it. He went on the offensive the moment that court proceedings began to snatch his great victory away from him. The families of his victims kept on choosing to interfere with his life, so he was going to interfere right back. He sent them letters and made phone calls, gloating over the awful things that he had done to their children. How he had enjoyed their bodies. How he had enjoyed their deaths. How he had tortured them. How they had begged for mercy and he had not given it to them. If the families wanted to fight him, he wanted them to know he would hold nothing back for their comfort. As one of the guards noted him saying, 'If I gave a damn about these families, I wouldn't have killed their kids.'

When open communication was cut off, Olson instead started passing his stories along to the papers, exclusively targeting the ones that served the areas where his victim's families lived. His campaign of terror worked. Several of the families pursuing legal action against him gave up and went away so that they didn't have to go on reliving the horror of their loss over and over.

Still, eventually some of them did get some measure of vengeance. Through civil courts, they sued Olson for injuries and losses, successfully scoring the full amount of his settlement as their payment, divided among the families still pursuing vengeance and the legal team that had finally won them this victory.

Unfortunately, there was no money to take. Olson had nothing himself. Not a penny to his name. The only money that had been involved in the case had been paid to his wife, who was an entirely separate legal entity. Legally, Olson may have owed the families $100,000, but there was no way that he could ever pay it. The whole exercise had been for nothing. He was bankrupt.

Still, the loss irked Olson, so he lashed out in the only way that he could: pointing out that he had been barred by the warden of the prison from writing and sending evidence into the court during the proceedings. This being the case, he had not been allowed to legally defend himself or instruct his lawyers to defend him. Of course, the warden had barred Olson from communication after he'd used it to torment his victims' families, but now it came back to bite him. Because his legal rights had been curtailed, the court judged that the Correctional Service of Canada was responsible for the costs that he had incurred. The families of his victims got their money, and he got to gloat at having taken it out of the pocket of the system that kept him confined. It was a win-win.

For a brief time, Olson fell silent in prison, sending out mail to the press and getting his odd moments in the spotlight but rarely making the front pages anymore. He wrote just as frequently to the justice department, offering up further bodies in exchange for more money or, latterly, for early parole. His offers were all unilaterally declined.

Out of the blue, he offered to travel to Vancouver Island and reveal the sites of more killings, no strings attached. He was driven around the backwoods, stopping at the same steakhouse he'd dined at during his first excursion with the police to wolf down some lunch before leading them on a wild goose chase for the remainder of the day. He'd been bored and fancied an outing. Growing bored with the stonewalling treatment he was receiving from his own country, Olson turned his attention south of the border, contacting the District Attorney for Washington State in the USA, offering up information regarding murders that he had committed there in exchange for immunity from prosecution. He worded these inquiries carefully to avoid anything that might be taken as an admission of guilt, as he was well aware that the death penalty was still alive and well in the USA, and eventually he did provide information that accounted for a series of bodies that had been discovered during his active period. Unlike his attempts to work with the Canadian authorities, his dealings with American police seemed to be primarily an exercise to avoid boredom. Similarly, he was set to assist police in Toronto with resolving a murder he had committed there in exchange for immunity for prosecution, but that eventually fell apart when they failed to offer him sufficient assurances. There seemed to be no self-serving pattern to this behaviour until his previous prison stays were taken into account. He was attempting to rebuild goodwill with his captors, trying to be seen as someone who could help them. Someone they could trust and reward.

Authorities in different countries also received mail from Olson as he tried to arrange for his extradition in exchange for information on further murders. Neither Switzerland nor any of the embassies he wrote to seemed interested.

Olson turned his focus to securing parole, claiming that he had made arrangements to write three books about his crimes, with millions in advances on offer, that he would happily disburse to the families of his victims if the parole panel could see to it that he was freed. Understandably, none of them leapt at this opportunity, and parole was denied. At every opportunity, he brought himself back in front of the parole board, and every single time he was denied. He had completely familiarised himself with the legal system of Canada, using every opportunity and loophole to try and secure his freedom, even testifying in his own defence, appealing to the public in the galleries who had gathered to watch his regularly scheduled circus, asking if he seemed like a raving madman. The public firmly responded that he did.

Gradually his campaigns for attention began to falter. The public had lost interest in him, the press were no longer publishing his letters, and without fresh controversy, he was fading into obscurity, barring one brief burst of notoriety in 2010 when it was discovered that he had been in receipt of substantial pension payments from the government, held in trust for him until he was free. This led to the Prime Minister, Stephen Harper, demanding an investigation that eventually terminated Olson's payments. Following that, Olson jokingly sent along one of his now-stopped cheques to Harper, asking that it be used for his re-election campaign. One last attempt at holding public attention before he was forgotten entirely.

In September of 2011, Olson was discovered to have terminal cancer. He was transferred to Laval Hospital in Quebec, where he survived only a few weeks before expiring at the age of 71, on the 30th of September.

Perfect Monster

From the age of seventeen, Clifford Olson Junior spent only 1,501 days outside of prison or jail. This is despite his constant escapes. Yet if his claims are to be believed, during those few days, he averaged about one murder every ten days. Tabulating all of the murders that he lays claim to, one hundred and forty sounds like a relatively likely maximum, but this is not accounting for those killings that he has simply never discussed. During his imprisonment, Clifford received a great deal of attention from criminologists and psychiatrists attempting to understand what had driven him to behave the way that he had throughout his life. During these interviews, he accounted for literally hundreds of molestations of children, admitted to committing necrophilia with his victims, and provided all of the information that, once corroborated with other sources, forms the basis of this book.

Psychologically, he seems to have been a classic psychopath, devoid of any remorse over his actions or even the capability of feeling such emotions. Many of the tools used to assess sociopathy were applied to him during his years of confinement, and interviews and studies of him even formed the basis for many methods of diagnosis of the condition.

There is a clinical checklist applied to rate the severity of psychopathy and the absence of empathy in a patient: The Hare checklist. When Clifford was assessed according to this list, he scored a 38 out of 40, the highest rating ever recorded. The standard threshold is 25 to 30.

Stanley Semrau was a forensic psychologist assigned to study Olson after his conviction, and his description of Clifford is a perfect match for every known definition of what a psychopath is. He could kill, not out of anger or upset, but for sport and amusement. He did not grasp the enormity and horror of his actions, because he was not capable of understanding the pain of others. In fact, his personality was devoted to harming and manipulating others to further his own interests. He was an anti-social, narcissistic psychopath who blithely boasted about his murders and exploits in interviews, deliberately manipulating everyone that he met and feeling no moral compunctions about anything that he did. He was described as being addicted to killing, with a morbid fascination about the death process, which he took great pleasure in observing. Any claims to remorse that he made were hollow attempts at manipulation, and he believed that the families of his victims owed him gratitude for revealing the locations of their bodies, likening it to World War 2, with Japan and Germany now being American allies when before they had been enemies. He couldn't understand why people couldn't just 'get over' his past crimes. In his own eyes, he had gone from being a nobody to a celebrity through the process of his murders and considered them to be a positive factor in his life. Semrau concluded that not only was Clifford a psychopath, but he was very content in being one. That he had absolutely no desire to change, and any appearance of change would invariably be another manipulation being used to extract some benefit.

While many serial killers suffer childhood trauma that could be understood as some sort of justification for their worldview, Olson had no defining moment in his history that resulted in his evil behaviour. There was no head injury that might have damaged the empathy centres of his brain, no physical reason that he might have turned out the way that he had. He came from a comfortable home, had siblings who grew up to be fully functional members of society. Whatever was wrong with him was entirely internal: a product of some defect of birth or a failure to develop the basic social skills that allowed humanity as a species to survive. He mimicked emotion but did not feel it. He could perfectly replicate philosophical debates, quote scripture and legal statutes, but inside none of these things connected. He could understand how laws and morals applied to other people, and he used those ties to manipulate them very easily, but none of it was for him. He was above good and evil. He was beyond the law. Quite simply, he was devoid of a conscience.

One final, parting anecdote about how Clifford saw the world. The film The Silence of the Lambs was screened at Olson's prison many years after its release, and one of the local reporters picked up on the parallels and went to ask Clifford about how he had enjoyed it.

When asked if he thought that he was comparable to the character of Hannibal Lecter, he replied, with a laugh, 'He's made up. I'm the real thing.'

THE BEAST

Want More?

Did you enjoy *The Beast* and want some more True Crime?

YOUR FREE BOOK IS WAITING

From bestselling author Ryan Green

There is a man who is officially classed as "**Britain's most dangerous prisoner**"

The man's name is Robert Maudsley, and his crimes earned him the nickname "**Hannibal the Cannibal**"

This free book is an exploration of his story...

 **nook** **kobo** **iBooks**

★★★★★   *"Ryan brings the horrifying details to life. I can't wait to read more by this author!"*

Get a free copy of ***Robert Maudsley: Hannibal the Cannibal*** when you sign up to join my Reader's Group.

www.ryangreenbooks.com/free-book

Every Review Helps

If you enjoyed the book and have a moment to spare, I would really appreciate a short review on Amazon. Your help in spreading the word is gratefully received and reviews make a huge difference to helping new readers find me. Without reviewers, us self-published authors would have a hard time!

Type in your link below to be taken straight to my book review page.

US	geni.us/BeastUS
UK	geni.us/BeastUK
Australia	geni.us/BeastAUS
Canada	geni.us/BeastCA

Thank you! I can't wait to read your thoughts.

About the Ryan Green

Ryan Green is a true crime author who lives in Herefordshire, England with his wife, three children, and two dogs. Outside of writing and spending time with his family, Ryan enjoys walking, reading and windsurfing.

Ryan is fascinated with History, Psychology and True Crime. In 2015, he finally started researching and writing his own work and at the end of the year, he released his first book on Britain's most notorious serial killer, Harold Shipman.

He has since written several books on lesser-known subjects, and taken the unique approach of writing from the killer's perspective. He narrates some of the most chilling scenes you'll encounter in the True Crime genre.

You can sign up to Ryan's newsletter to receive a free book, updates, and the latest releases at:

WWW.RYANGREENBOOKS.COM

More Books by Ryan Green

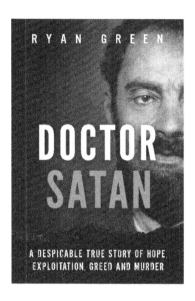

In 1944, as the Nazis occupied Paris, the French Police and Fire Brigade were called to investigate a vile-smelling smoke pouring out from a Parisian home. Inside, they were confronted with a scene from a nightmare. They found a factory line of bodies and multiple furnaces stocked with human remains. This was more than mere murder .

The homeowner was Dr. Marcel Petiot, an admired and charismatic physician. When questioned, Dr. Petiot claimed that he was a part of the Resistance and the bodies they discovered belonged to Nazi collaborators that he killed for the cause. The French Police, resentful of Nazi occupation and confused by a rational alternative, allowed him to leave.

Was the respected Doctor a clandestine hero fighting for national liberty or a deviant using dire domestic circumstances to his advantage? One thing is for certain, the Police and the Nazis both wanted to get their hands on Dr. Marcel Petiot to find out the truth.

More Books by Ryan Green

On 20 May 1999, the South Australian Police were called to investigate a disued bank in the unassuming town of Snowtown, in connection to the disappearance of multiple missing people. The Police were not prepared for the chilling scene that awaited them.

The officers found six barrels within the abandoned bank vault, each filled with acid and the remains of eight individuals. Accompanying the bodies were numerous everyday tools that pathologists would later confirm were used for prolonged torture, murder and cannibalism.

The findings shocked Australia to its core, which deepened still when it was revealed that the torture and murders were committed by not one, but a group of killers. The four men, led by John Bunting, targeted paedophiles, homosexuals, addicts or the 'weak' in an attempt to cleanse society.

More Books by Ryan Green

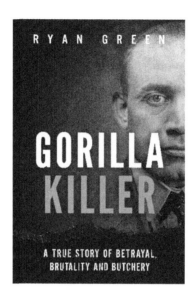

On 20th February 1926, landlady Clara Newman (60) opened her door to a potential tenant who enquired into the availability of one of her rooms. Despite his grim and bulky appearance, he introduced himself politely, in a soft-spoken voice whilst clutching a Bible in one of his large hands. She invited him in. The moment he stepped into her home, he lunged forwards, wrapping his over-sized fingers around her throat and forced her to the ground. She couldn't scream. He had learned the dangers of a scream. She slowly slipped into darkness. Given what would follow, it was probably a kindness.

The 'Gorilla Killer', Earle Nelson, roamed over 7,000 miles of North America undetected, whilst satisfying his deranged desires. During a span of almost two years, he choked the life out of more than twenty unsuspecting women, subjected their bodies to the most unspeakable acts, and seemingly enjoyed the process.

More Books by Ryan Green

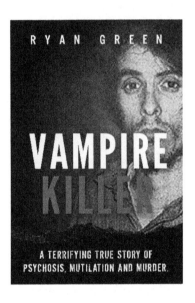

On 23 January 1978, David Wallin returned to an unlit home. His pregnant wife, Teresa (22), was nowhere to be seen. The radio was still playing and there were some peculiar stains on the carpet. Wallin nervously followed the stains to his bedroom and encountered a scene so chilling that it would haunt him for the rest of his life. Teresa had been sexually assaulted and mutilated. She was also missing body parts and large volumes of blood.

Four days later, the Sacramento Police Department were called to a home approximately a mile away from the Wallin residence. They were not prepared for the horror that awaited them. Daniel Meredith (56) and Jason Miroth (6) were shot multiple times. Evelyn Miroth (38) was disfigured, disembowelled and abused like Teresa. She was also missing body parts and large quantities of blood. David Ferreira (2), who Evelyn was babysitting, was nowhere to be seen and likely in the hands of the deranged mass murderer.

Free True Crime Audiobook

Listen to four chilling True Crime stories in one collection. Follow the link below to download a FREE copy of *The Ryan Green True Crime Collection: Vol. 3.*

WWW.RYANGREENBOOKS.COM/FREE-AUDIOBOOK

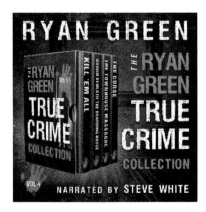

"Ryan Green has produced another excellent book and belongs at the top with true crime writers such as M. William Phelps, Gregg Olsen and Ann Rule" –**B.S. Reid**

"Wow! Chilling, shocking and totally riveting! I'm not going to sleep well after listening to this but the narration was fantastic. Crazy story but highly recommend for any true crime lover!" –**Mandy**

"Torture Mom by Ryan Green left me pretty speechless. The fact that it's a true story is just...wow" –**JStep**

"Graphic, upsetting, but superbly read and written" –**Ray C**

WWW.RYANGREENBOOKS.COM/FREE-AUDIOBOOK

Printed in Great Britain
by Amazon

27532798R00078